ORIENTEERING IN THE NATIONAL CURRICULUM

Published 1992 by

HARVEYS
12-16 Main Street
Doune, Perthshire FK16 6BJ
Tel: 0786 841202
Fax: 0786 841098

ISBN 1 85137 005 6

Acknowledgements

Cover photo:
Anthony Wright

Children in photo:
Victoria Junior School, Barrow-in-Furness

Cover map:
Based on the map of Denny High School
© Central Regional Council

Lesson plan illustrations:
Ian Whalley

Contents

Foreword

Orienteering with children has been a central part of my life for thirty years. In the early 1960s my Surrey pupils used black and white photocopies of the 1:25,000 Ordnance Survey map to locate painted biscuit tins on local commons. The word 'orienteering' meant nothing to the great majority of the British school population.

We now have five-colour redrawn maps, permanent courses and well tried teaching schemes that avoid the traumas of getting badly lost, but orienteering retains the same basic magic. The thrill of sighting the small orange and white marker through the trees touches the David Livingstone in all of us.

This publication attempts to give every teacher sufficient information and ideas to enable him/her both to open up the 'magic' for many more children and at the same time to use orienteering as a practical means for developing a variety of skills across the National Curriculum.

In supporting this imaginative venture, the British Orienteering Federation knows that not only will generations of children be led into a rich educational environment, but that with expert teaching, many will continue to explore the variety of experiences which orienteering has to offer.

Peter Palmer

Director of Coaching 1989-92
British Orienteering Federation

1   Introduction

Orienteering is basically a simple sport in which competitors navigate round a series of checkpoints using a large-scale map and sometimes a compass. The kit is simple - just sensible outdoor clothes, a pair of trainers with 'grip' and a clear polythene bag to use as a map case. Although the fastest back wins, navigational skills are more important than running speed and the competition is often more with self than others.

Like all sports, success demands a mastery of basic skills - map orientation, pacing, distance judgement, etc - but, unlike many sports, orienteering can take a variety of forms. It can be performed recreationally or competitively by all ages and levels of technical and physical ability. Whether cross-country, score, line, relay or a 'trail' event, it still combines the essential elements of navigation, decision making and activity - and above all, remains fun.

It can take place in the classroom, in school grounds, or in woodland. Courses can take a couple of hours or a few minutes and competitors can walk, run, ride a mountain bike or even paddle a canoe if the opportunity exists. The basic criteria are that maps must be large scale and accurate, the control points must be identifiable by skill and not luck, and the emphasis in course planning should be on following a chosen route successfully and not in looking for a hidden control marker. Orienteering can be a treasure hunt only if the treasure is located solely by applied skill. Experience shows that children introduced to the sport by a positive system which builds on confidence are much more likely to continue than those haunted by fears of getting lost.

Orienteering started in Sweden about 80 years ago. Today, Scandinavian events attract many thousands of participants and "orienteering and the outdoor life" is a compulsory element within the Swedish National Curriculum. In a large country of which four-fifths is forest, it is important that its citizens can find their way about confidently, particularly during the summer months when many Swedes emerge from winter 'hibernation' to enjoy the countryside. Free access to the countryside (Allemansrätt) is every citizen's birthright, and a healthy lifestyle means lower health bills.

The sport came to Britain in the late 1950's. Since then it has grown steadily, and now

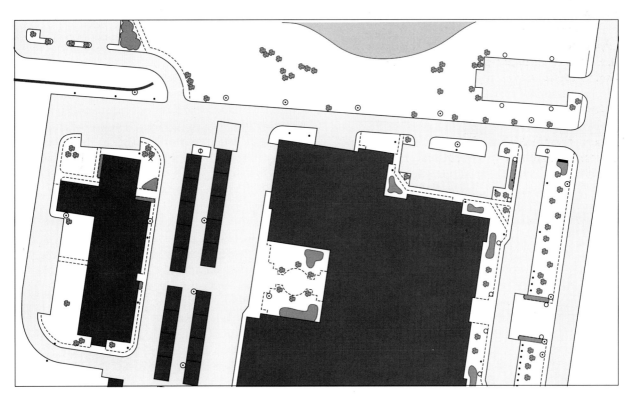

there is a full programme of events across the country most weekends. Thousands of children have been introduced to its various dimensions through Outdoor Education schemes and intra- and extra-curricular activities in individual schools. The British Schools Championships regularly attract well over a thousand entrants from all over the UK. The sport is controlled and governed by the British Orienteering Federation.

There are already well-tried systems for progressing children's orienteering from classroom to campus and local park. The practical emphasis on map reading and route finding within the Geography National Curriculum and the inclusion of Outdoor Adventure activities in the PE Curriculum have now given a new dimension to educational orienteering. Nor are these the only curricular areas where orienteering has direct relevance. Because it involves map scales, direction and measurement, mathematics comes into the picture, while problem-solving brings in personal education, communication and language. The countryside introduces the environment, new locations mean adventure, while the organisation of orienteering activities and provision of equipment involve design and technology. The guide which follows explores all these cross-curricular links as well as identifying the key areas of orienteering input.

Orienteering thus offers a creative but inexpensive outdoor activity on the school site or close by, but understandably, many busy teachers see it as complicated, time-consuming and difficult to set up. This book sets out to allay those fears by relating orienteering activities to identified curriculum areas and by giving clear guidance on how to plan lessons and assess results, as well as providing resource information and references to more detailed publications. It concentrates on effective use of the immediate school environment and, while prescriptive in approach, it leaves teachers free to adapt the lesson plans to individual schemes of work or personal areas of interest. It pursues, step by step, the well researched orienteering teaching system of orientated map (by compass or ground), the following of 'line feature' routes, and progression from classroom to the wider world. Teachers are free to decide when and how to introduce specific activities or to assess how much weight to give to competitive activity as against group work, map-making or environmental interest. Similarly, teachers themselves can decide how far to involve children in making basic equipment such as control markers and how far to use commercial suppliers. As part of a community studies project, one school recently designed and set up a permanent course with a newly drawn map and fixed control posts on a disused mining site. The mapping, construction and negotiation involved Geography,

Maths, Technology, Environmental Studies, Social Education, Language and some local history, while physical fitness was called for in the competition organised for the official opening.

The arrangement of this guide is straightforward. It is intended for practising teachers and instructors in outdoor education centres and it therefore assumes a working knowledge of the National Curriculum. It deals only with Key Stages 1 and 2; a companion guide for Key Stages 3 and 4 will follow.

This introduction is followed by an examination of areas within the National Curriculum where there are clear opportunities to use orienteering activities within study pro- grammes. It then moves on to provide a series of practical ideas and lesson plans that are related to specific areas. A framework of assessment suggests a way of recording progress. Short chapters follow that suggest extensions beyond school for those teachers or children who wish to pursue their interest further. The guide concludes with appendices containing sample maps and resource information. Above all, it is intended to provide teachers with simple, useful information on how to use orienteering realistically as a practical vehicle for delivering attainment targets within the National Curriculum.

Finally, whichever path you take through the orienteering 'forest', we hope that like us, you will enjoy the pleasure of seeing children grow in self-confidence and awareness as they develop their interest in this fascinating activity. We can guarantee that, whatever your objectives at the start of your orienteering journey into the Nat- ional Curriculum, you will explore many byways and diversions en route that would not have presented themselves at the start.

2 How orienteering relates to the National Curriculum

THEMES	Health Education
	Environmental Education
	Economic & Industrial Understanding
	Education for Citizenship
	Careers Education & Guidance

SKILLS	Communication
	Numeracy
	Graphicacy
	Problem Solving
	Study Skills
	Information Handling Skills

SUBJECTS

English
Mathematics
Science

Technology

Geography & History

Art, Music & Physical Education

DIMENSIONS	Multicultural Considerations
	Gender Issues
	Special Education Needs

Aspects of the National Curriculum

INTRODUCTION

In this chapter we show how different forms of orienteering relate to the National Curriculum. We discuss how involvement in small scale events draws the different subject areas together into a cohesive project which not only teaches facts, skills and knowledge but also inculcates positive attitudes and values. The chapter concludes with a rationale for teaching orienteering, and raises questions to be addressed as a form of assessment, points which are followed up in Chapter 5.

ASPECTS OF THE NATIONAL CURRICULUM

The National Curriculum consists of a number of subjects, though not all are given equal weight. The core reflects the 'old basics' of mathematics and English, to which has been added the relatively new subject (for primary schools) of science. Technology forms a second tier with geography and history adding the third layer. Art, music and physical education complete the steps.

It presents an adventure activity on the school's doorstep

It's real problem solving

It's useful

It's challenging

It's a good leisure activity

It develops life skills

It opens children's horizons to a new sport

It's decision making

It's enjoyable

It's fun

It's motivating

It builds self confidence and independence

It's map and compass

Everyone can do it

It gives children confidence to find their way

It provides purpose and relevance to learning

It builds health and fitness in an individual way

It uses the real world rather than exercises in books

It links mathematics and geography

It gets you out of the classroom

It gets children talking

It enables children to observe their environment

It answers PE and Outdoor Adventure Education cost effectively

What teachers say about orienteering as a topic for delivering the National Curriculum

The relative importance of the subjects is reflected in the order in which they have been introduced into the Curriculum. With the publication of the Statutory Orders for art, music and physical education in September 1992, all the subjects are in place.

However, subject knowledge alone cannot deliver the National Curriculum. Three cross-curricular elements have been added in an attempt to tie the basic curriculum together. These three elements are termed skills, dimensions and themes and, though non-statutory, they cover important areas of knowledge and understanding and are intended to permeate the whole curriculum.

The skills were originally called 'competencies' and include communication, numeracy and graphicacy skills, problem solving, information handling and study skills. Themes, such as health education, environmental education and citizenship, show how close links can be made with subjects, while the dimensions relate to personal and social education as well as addressing bias and discrimination.

THEORY INTO ACTION

The basic challenge for the busy primary teacher is that of translating the theory of the National Curriculum into action. Although the subjects themselves may be seen as separate entities, the programmes of study do overlap.

Furthermore, the subject hierarchy and associated assessment tasks could severely limit the time available for subjects such as history and geography. Time constraints can be alleviated by combining areas of the curriculum, but the separate programmes of study in their individually coloured ring binders neither assist nor motivate teachers to draw the necessary threads and connections which exist between them.

It is also true that the statements to be covered can appear prescriptive and complex, requiring specialist knowledge. Although the programmes of study should not be seen as 'set in stone', or rigidly matched to the age and needs of every child, some teachers understandably find it difficult to deliver the curriculum effectively, particularly from a cross-curricular perspective.

This need not be the case, and a study of orienteering can help to link core and foundation subjects and embrace skills, themes and dimensions. Reactions from teachers who have tried the materials provides many positive comments about the value of orienteering. How does this come about?

FINDING THE WAY

Orienteering is a sport in which a map and compass are used to decide on a route to a precise destination, at which there is a control marker. The skills involved are similar in many ways to those used in everyday life when using a map, whether walking or driving. A clearer understanding of the techniques involved will allow children and adults to become more confident in their use of maps.

The challenge of orienteering is that of solving the route choice problem efficiently and speedily in order to reach the precise destination (the control marker). The practical value of a knowledge of map and compass skills rapidly becomes apparent. It is not about learning cardinal points, symbols or grid references for their own sake, but more about relating the map and compass to the terrain and in turn, noticing features on the ground which can be located on the map. Orienteering thus uses two important tools, the map and the compass, knowledge of which will be useful in fieldwork, both in the local environment and in the wider world.

So where do we start? First with a simple map of the classroom, the hall, the gymnasium, playground, school field or local park. The map should be clear, large scale and the features on it should be correct in the depiction of size and relationship to each other.

The lesson plans detail how such maps can be produced, but let us assume for the moment that the pupil understands the concept of a map, can recognise plan view and understands the notion of a key. What questions then confront the young navigator? As they arise, consider not only their importance but also whether they are covered by conventional mapwork teaching and exercises. The questions centre around four important ideas: orientation, route choice, map contact and location.

Key questions to ask yourself when navigating

ORIENTATION:
Is the map the right way round?
Does the map match the ground?
How can I use landmarks to set the map?
How do I use the compass to set the map?
Note: You can always set the map with a compass, but only sometimes by using landmarks.

ROUTE CHOICE:
Where am I now?
Can I find this point on the map?
Where am I going?
Which way can I go?
Are there any other possible routes?

ROUTE CHOICE (continued)

Are there obstacles or difficulties on my route?

Which route is shortest?

Which route is quickest?

Which route is easiest?

Which route is best?

How far is it?

How long will I take?

In which direction do I set off?

STAYING ON ROUTE:

How do I know I'm still on route?

What will I notice and check off on my route?

How will I know when I'm near my destination?

How can I keep a check on my position?

What skills do I need to do all this well?

ON ARRIVAL:

Did my plan work out in action?

Did I find the destination precisely?

Was the route a good one?

Did I meet unexpected problems?

Could my route have been simpler or quicker?

Was I hesitant or confident?

Did I need to keep checking the map?

Did I map read accurately?

Did I use the compass?

Did I take note of distance?

How long did I take?

How pleased was I with my performance?

Can the answers to these important questions be located within the National Curriculum at Key Stages 1 and 2?

The answer is yes. Principally, the activities match skills in the geography programmes of study. For example, using maps of routes and small areas, interpreting symbols, directional skills, describing location, identifying features and using a compass. Similarly, the activities relate to the use and application of mathematics (AT1) and to Shape and Space (AT4), as many key concepts such as distance, direction, location, shape, scale, links and networks are shared with geography.

The sport of orienteering readily fits into outdoor and adventurous education, while its specific techniques can form games and athletic activity. Finally, after any act of navigation or wayfinding you inevitably talk to others about the experience. The ability to recall and describe your route, and how you travelled along it, provide opportunities for English.

GEOGRAPHY

AT1 Geographical Skills
   (i) The use of maps
   (ii) Fieldwork techniques
AT2 Knowledge & understanding of places
AT5 Environmental Geography

MATHEMATICS

AT1 Using and applying mathematics
   (i) In practical tasks
   (ii) Real life problem solving
AT4 Shape and Space
   (i) Use measurement and location
      in the study of space

ORIENTEERING:
ROUTE PROBLEM SOLVING
"FINDING YOUR WAY"

Specific requirements:
   (i) Athletic activity
   (ii) Games
   (iii) Outdoor and adventurous activities
General requirement:
   Physical activity

PHYSICAL EDUCATION

AT1 Speaking and listening
AT3 Writing

ENGLISH

The Skills of Orienteering and Links with Core and Foundation Subjects

TYPES OF ORIENTEERING

One of the values of orienteering is that it can take many forms. The same familiar area can be used repeatedly to extend the range of skills and experience while providing a secure setting for the pupil, and thus raising confidence. In our experience children soon begin to want to run, rather than walk, and so competition, both against yourself and others, becomes a natural extension.

Orienteering is a sport of physical and mental challenge, usually undertaken on an individual basis, but there are also opportunities for group activities and team events. The different forms of orienteering set out here form a whole succession and range of exercises to practice and develop map and compass skills within the school grounds.

Cross-country

In the basic competitive form of orienteering, a course is completed by visiting a number of control points in a set order. The winner is the person who correctly completes the course in the shortest time. Courses can be circular or crossover in design.

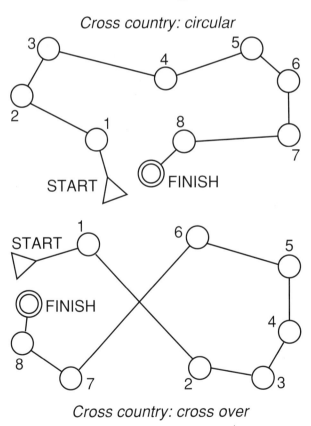

Cross country: circular

Cross country: cross over

Score orienteering

In score events, a large number of controls are set out and each is given a points value, depending on degree of difficulty and distance from the start. A set time is given to collect as

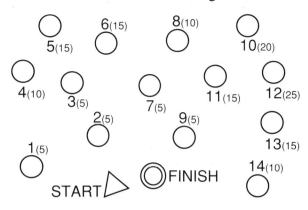

Score orienteering

many control points as possible, with a scale of penalty points being deducted for late return.

In team score events, teams of two, three or four work together to collect the controls. Decisions have to be made within the time allocation as to who goes for which controls. Again, a set time limit is given and there are penalties for being late back.

Relay orienteering

Relays are fun and exert time pressure as well as team responsibility on competitors. Teams are normally of three, and the map is used as a type of baton. There are several variations on how the courses can be set out. In some events, 'common controls' are used on all courses, to increase interest for both competitors and spectators, as this enables race progress to be judged.

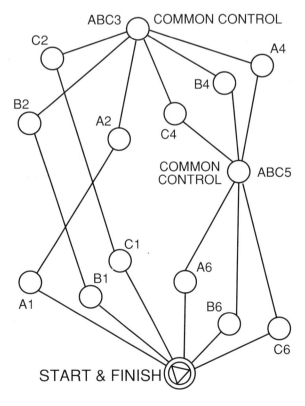

Relay orienteering

Do they...
Observe features, note what is where?
Discuss what the place is like?
Discuss direction, location, scale?
Discuss reaction to a place?
Think - why is this place like this?
Respond to a place?
Respond actively?

GEOGRAPHY
AT1 Geographical Skills
        (i) The use of maps
        (ii) Fieldwork techniques
AT2 Knowledge & understanding of places
AT5 Environmental Geography

Do they... develop the ability to tackle problems?
Use mathematics effectively?
Work independently? Work collaboratively?
Work as a team? Evaluate solutions?
Use mathematical tools (compass) with confidence?
Estimate results in advance?
Persevere?
Are they.. motivated
to have a go?
Accurate?
Systematic?
Willing to check?

MATHEMATICS
AT1 Using and applying mathematics
        (i) In practical tasks
        (ii) Real life problem solving
AT4 Shape and Space
        (i) Use measurement and location
            in the study of space

ORIENTEERING:
ROUTE PROBLEM SOLVING
"FINDING YOUR WAY"

Do they...
Follow rules?
Respond readily
    to instructions?
Become aware of
    the effect of their
    actions on
    (a) others (b) the environment?
Observe fair play, honest competition?
Act in a sporting manner?
Cope with success and failure?
Learn skills and practise?
Learn to evaluate their initial attempts and
    decide how to modify subsequent attempts?

Specific requirements:
        (i) Athletic activity
        (ii) Games
        (iii) Outdoor and adventurous activities
General requirement:
        Physical activity
PHYSICAL EDUCATION

AT1 Speaking and listening
AT3 Writing
ENGLISH

Do they...
Listen:
hear explanations,
instructions,
questions
and answers?

Talk:
make predictions, ask questions,
talk through difficulties, report outcomes
use relevant language?

Reflect:
upon outcomes, strategies and actions?

Observing children orienteering: personal reactions, attitudes and qualities

Many practices and activities can be used in preparation for the above variations. We have set out a suggested sequence of lesson plans in Chapter 4.

Collaborative efforts under time and distance pressure present real challenges and so orienteering can be used to see not only whether the navigational problems are solved, but also how they are solved.

The diagram 'Observing children orienteering' (above) shows statements from the non-statutory guidance of the National Curriculum in Geography, English, Mathematics and PE. It has been designed to provide a list of questions which can be foremost in the teacher's mind when observing the children at work either individually or collaboratively.

The statements contain elements which cohesive schemes of work should possess together with the qualities, attitudes and values to be generated. There is considerable overlap between subjects, but equally there are distinctions. Mathematics illustrates the skills and attitudes required in problem-solving while physical education emphasises playing your part and obeying rules. Both subjects encourage practice

and reflection, which is also apparent in the discussion element of English.

Geography is not just a study of place but also how you react to it, not just features on maps and photographs but how you feel about being there. To orienteer, first within the school grounds and then in wider areas, can lead to an examination of how you feel about measures of security, the enjoyment of success, the feeling of failure, the disappointment of underachievement or the general wellbeing of having played your part within a particular context. All these affect our understanding of place.

3 Programmes of study

MATHEMATICS AND ORIENTEERING IN THE NATIONAL CURRICULUM

USING AND APPLYING MATHEMATICS   ATTAINMENT TARGET 1

PROGRAMME OF STUDY	STATEMENT OF ATTAINMENT	EXAMPLES IN ORIENTEERING
Pupils should engage in activities which involve:	Pupils should be able to:	Pupils could:
LEVEL 1		
• using materials for a practical task • talking about their work and asking questions	• use mathematics as an integral part of practical classroom tasks 1b. talk about their own work and respond to questions 1c. make predictions, etc.	• count models used for desk top plans • discuss shapes of models • talk about size of shapes used as symbols for models or apparatus
LEVEL 2		
• asking and responding to questions, eg "What would happen if ...? Why ...?"	2a. make and put out a control marker 2b. talk about work using appropriate mathematical language 2c. respond appropriately to the question "What would happen if ...?"	• discuss relationship of child to desk top models depending on which side they look at it. The house is in front of the wall, the tree is beside the house . .
LEVEL 3		
• explaining work and recording findings systematically	3a. find ways of overcoming difficulties in problem solving 3b. use or interpret appropriate mathematical terms and mathematical aspects of everyday language in a precise way	• learn how to travel on a route • record letters from numbered orienteering control markers
LEVEL 4		
• selecting the materials and the mathematics to use for a task when the information leaves opportunities for choice and for planning work methodically • recording findings and presenting them in oral, written or visual form	4a. identify and obtain information necessary to solve problems 4b. interpret situations mathematically, using appropriate symbols or diagrams 4d. make generalisations	• discuss what information is needed to find a control • draw classroom or playground maps to scale • time a competition and put the results in correct order • generate strategies for cross country and score events
LEVEL 5		
• selecting the materials and the mathematics to use for a task; checking there is sufficient information; working methodically and reviewing progress • breaking tasks into smaller, more manageable sections • interpreting mathematical information presented in oral, written or visual form	5a. carry through a task by breaking it down into smaller, more manageable sections 5b. interpret information presented in a variety of mathematical forms 5c. make a generalisation and test it	• plan a short course • solve a route choice problem • decide on score values for control points in score orienteering • discuss the use of scale for plans and maps • discuss how it feels to cover a specific distance on the ground measured from the map • test that the most direct route is not always the quickest • test strategies for aiming off

MATHEMATICS AND ORIENTEERING IN THE NATIONAL CURRICULUM

NUMBER   ATTAINMENT TARGET 2

PROGRAMME OF STUDY	STATEMENT OF ATTAINMENT	EXAMPLES IN ORIENTEERING
Pupils should engage in activities which involve:	*Pupils should be able to:*	*Pupils could:*
LEVEL 1		
• counting, reading, writing and ordering numbers to at least 10 • learning that the size of a set is given by the last number in the count • understanding language associated with number, e.g. 'more', 'fewer', 'the same' • understanding conservation of number • making a sensible estimate of a number of objects up to 10 • using addition and subtraction, with numbers no greater that 10, in the context of real objects	1a. use number in the context of the classroom and school 1b. add and subtract using a small number of objects	• count control points • count models on apparatus • find 3 controls from 5 • select a number of models to draw a desk top plan
LEVEL 2		
• knowing and using addition and subtraction facts up to 100 • reading, writing and ordering numbers to at least 100 and using the knowledge that the 10s digit indicates the number of 10s • solving whole-number problems involving addition and subtraction, including money • using non-standard measures in length, area, capacity, weight and time; comparing objects and events and recognising the need for standard units	2a. demonstrate that they know and can use number facts, including addition and subtraction 2b. solve whole-number problems involving addition and subtraction 2c. identify halves and quarters 2d. recognise the need for standard units of measurement	• calculate the maximum points possible in a score event • discuss how drawing objects to scale solves the problem of not being able to accommodate them (life-size) on a sheet of paper • relate rotation to cardinal points • discuss rotation and identify features on half and quarter rotations
LEVEL 3		
• reading, writing and ordering numbers up to at least 1000, and using the knowledge that the position of a digit indicates its value • learning and using addition and subtraction facts to 20 (including zero) • learning and using multiplication facts up to 5 x 5 and all those in the 2, 5 and 10 multiplication tables • making estimates based on familiar units • recognising that the first digit is the most important in indicating the size of a number and approximating to the nearest 10 or 100	3a. read, write and order numbers up to 1000 3b. demonstrate that they know and can use multiplication tables 3d. make estimates based on familiar units of measurement, checking results	• estimate distance on a map, e.g. on a 1:5000 map, 1cm = 50 metres • use a pacing scale • estimate distance in the playground - how far is the wall from the building? • measure and compare estimation of angles and bearings using half, quarter and eighth turns in a clockwise direction
LEVEL 4		
• reading, writing and ordering whole numbers • learning multiplication facts up to 10 x 10 and using them in multiplication and division problems • adding and subtracting mentally two two-digit numbers	4a. solve problems without the aid of a calculator, considering the reasonableness of the answer 4c. make sensible estimates of a range of measures	• subtract start time from finish time to calculate time taken • put times into the correct order • estimate direction in degrees • estimate distance
LEVEL 5		
• understanding the notion of scale in maps and drawings	5b. find fractions or percentages of quantities 5d. use units in context	• use the scale of a map to measure distance then follow the chosen route • discuss the units of measurement of scale on a map • use appropriate units for rough and fine orienteering

MATHEMATICS AND ORIENTEERING IN THE NATIONAL CURRICULUM

SHAPE AND SPACE   ATTAINMENT TARGET 4

PROGRAMME OF STUDY	STATEMENT OF ATTAINMENT	EXAMPLES IN ORIENTEERING
Pupils should engage in activities which involve:	Pupils should be able to:	Pupils could:
LEVEL 1		
• sorting and classifying 2-D and 3-D shapes using words such as "straight", "flat", "curved", "round", "pointed", etc. • building 3-D solid shapes and drawing 2-D shapes and describing them • using common words, such as "on", "inside", "above", "under", "behind", "next to", to describe a position • giving and understanding instructions for movement along a route • comparing objects and ordering objects and events without measuring, using appropriate language	1a. talk about models they have made 1b. follow or give instructions related to movement and position 1c. compare and order objects without measuring	• describe the plan they have made from models • describe their 'treasure island' and the route they would take to find the treasure • use common words to describe the pattern and routes on a picture map
LEVEL 2		
• recognising squares, rectangles, circles, triangles, hexagons, pentagons, cubes, rectangular boxes (cuboids), cylinders and spheres and describing their properties • recognising right-angled corners in 2-D and 3-D shapes • recognising types of movement: straight (translation), turning (rotation) • understanding angle as a measurement of turn • understanding turning through right angles • understanding the conservation of length, capacity and 'weight'	2a. use mathematical terms to describe common 2-D shapes and 3-D objects 2b. recognise different types of movement	• use desk top plans and picture maps • describe models for a plan using appropriate language • use language of rotation when following a route
LEVEL 3		
• sorting 2-D and 3-D shapes and giving reasons for each method of sorting • recognising (reflective) symmetry in a variety of shapes in two and three dimensions • using and understanding compass bearings and the terms 'clockwise' and 'anti-clockwise'	3a. sort shapes using mathematical criteria and give reasons 3b. recognise reflective symmetry 3c. use the eight points of the compass to show direction	• relate symbol shapes to the features they represent e.g. school buildings, apparatus • draw plans and matching patterns with 3D features • know where north is in the area used for orienteering
LEVEL 4		
• understanding and using language associated with angle • specifying location by means of co-ordinates in the first quadrant and by means of angle and distance	4a. construct 2-D or 3-D shapes and know associated language 4b. specify location	• understand turning to face a new direction keeping the map set - predicting the angle of turn from the map • keep map contact whilst orienteering
LEVEL 5		
• using networks to solve problems	5a. use networks to solve problems	• discuss route choice problems - which is the shortest route using paths?
LEVEL 6		
• understanding and using bearings to define direction	6c. use and understand bearings to show direction	• solve a route problem using rough and fine bearings, aiming off & safety bearings

15

MATHEMATICS AND ORIENTEERING IN THE NATIONAL CURRICULUM

HANDLING DATA   ATTAINMENT TARGET 5

PROGRAMME OF STUDY	STATEMENT OF ATTAINMENT	EXAMPLES IN ORIENTEERING
Pupils should engage in activities which involve:	Pupils should be able to:	Pupils could:
LEVEL 1		
• creating simple mapping diagrams showing relationships and interpreting them	1a. sort a set of objects, describing the criteria chosen	• use desk top plans
LEVEL 2		
• choosing criteria to sort and classify objects, recording results or outcomes of events	2a. interpret relevant data which has been collected	• record results from an orienteering event
• designing a data collection sheet, collecting and recording data, leading to a frequency table		• decide whether individuals should be listed separately from pairs, or boys separate from girls
LEVEL 3		
• extracting specific pieces of information from tables and lists • entering and accessing information in a simple database • entering data into a simple database and using it to find answers to simple questions	3a. access information in a simple database	• make a start list for a small event and discuss categories of age and sex • print out result list •find out which controls were not visited on a score course
LEVEL 4		
• inserting, interrogating and interpreting data in a computer database	4a. interrogate and interpret data in a computer database	• use a computer database to record results and calculate speed
• specifying an issue for which data is needed	4b. conduct a survey on an issue of their choice	• devise a table for recording improvement in speed of running or orienteering
• collecting, grouping and ordering discrete data using tallying methods and creating a frequency table for grouped data.		• calculate average distance, points, time, speed
LEVEL 6		
• specifying an issue for which data is needed; designing and using observation sheets to collect data; collating and analysing results	6a. design and use a questionnaire to survey opinion	• design a questionnaire to survey reaction to an event or participation in a trim course
• designing and using a questionnaire to survey opinion		
• collating and analysing results		

PHYSICAL EDUCATION WITH OUTDOOR AND ADVENTUROUS ACTIVITIES AND ORIENTEERING IN THE NATIONAL CURRICULUM

KEY STAGE 1: LEVELS 1-3

PROGRAMME OF STUDY	STATEMENT OF ATTAINMENT	EXAMPLES IN ORIENTEERING
General Pupils should: • be made aware of the changes that happen to their bodies during exercise	Pupils should be able to: • practise and improve performance 1d. recognise the effects of physical activity on their body • describe what they and others are doing	Pupils could: • run legs of a course • describe the route and their way of travel • detect that their heart beats faster, breathing is more rapid and that they become hotter during exercise
Athletic Activity Pupils should: • experience and take part in running		
Outdoor and Adventurous Activities Pupils should: • explore the potential for physical activities within the immediate environment • undertake simple orientation tasks • develop an awareness of basic safety practices		Pupils could: • practise orienteering games and exercises in the school hall and playground • try 'Look before you run'. Reading a map well means you can find your way and not get lost so easily.

PHYSICAL EDUCATION WITH OUTDOOR AND ADVENTUROUS ACTIVITIES AND ORIENTEERING IN THE NATIONAL CURRICULUM

KEY STAGE 2: LEVELS 2-5

PROGRAMME OF STUDY	*STATEMENT OF ATTAINMENT*	*EXAMPLES IN ORIENTEERING*
General *Pupils should:* • be enabled to respond quickly to changing environments or adjust to other people's actions	*Pupils should be able to:* 2b. perform effectively in activities requiring quick decision-making	*Pupils could:* • practise quick decision-making during competitive orienteering games - where am I? - which way do I go? - what do I follow?
• be given opportunities to work alone to ensure the development of their own personal skills	2c. respond safely, alone and with others, to challenging tasks taking account of levels of skill and understanding	• use star exercises to encourage working alone in an unfamiliar area. Every child always has his/her own map
• be taught to help themselves to improve by making simple comments and judgements on their own performance and that of others	2e. evaluate how well they and others perform and behave against criteria suggested by the teacher, and suggest ways of improving performance	• find control points in a limited time - score orienteering • practise, listen, watch, help others in order to improve. Analyse performance to show areas of skill which need improvement • go running and orienteering whenever possible. Recognise improvement of skills through practice
• be taught to understand the value of and demonstrate sustained activity over appropriate periods of time	2f. sustain energetic activity over appropriate periods of time in a range of physical activities and understand the effects of exercise on the body	• use orienteering to observe changes in pulse rate, breathing, body temperature. Heart muscles will adapt to exercise and become more efficient. Fitness is increased
• be taught to understand the immediate and short term effects of exercise on the body		• learn to wear appropriate clothing, and not to eat or drink before running. Gentle use of muscles and joints before any fast activity - 'warm up the engine before driving it fast'. Keep warm after activity. Shower. Change clothes
• be taught to understand and demon-strate how to prepare for particular activities and how to recover afterwards		
Athletic Activity *Pupils should:* • practise and develop basic actions in running		*Pupils could:* • run in different terrains
• experience competitions including those they make up themselves		• experience cross country, score, line and relay events
Outdoor and Adventurous Activities *Pupils should:* • learn the principles of safety in the outdoors and develop the ability to assess and respond to challenges in a variety of contexts and conditions		• learn about safety bearings, emergency whistle signal, what to do when lost, re-porting to the finish, appropriate clothing
• experience outdoor and adventurous activities in different environments (such as school grounds, parks or woodland) that involve planning, navigation, working in small groups, recording and evaluating		• learn responsible behaviour - care of the environment, care of each other. Fair play - no cheating. Care of activity - do not move control markers • go orienteering in school grounds, parks or woodland, organise an orienteering event, analyse individual performance
• be taught the skills necessary for the activity undertaken with due regard for safety including the correct use of appropriate equipment		• learn that skilful use of map and com-pass in orienteering gives knowledge and experience needed to navigate anywhere

GEOGRAPHY AND ORIENTEERING IN THE NATIONAL CURRICULUM

GEOGRAPHICAL SKILLS   ATTAINMENT TARGET 1

PROGRAMME OF STUDY	STATEMENT OF ATTAINMENT	EXAMPLES IN ORIENTEERING
Enquiry should form an important part of pupils' work in geography in Key Stage 1. Work should be linked to pupils' own interests, experience and capabilities and should lead to investigations based on fieldwork and classroom activities. Much of pupils' learning in Key Stage 1 should be based on direct experience, practical activities and exploration of the local area		
Pupils should be taught to:	*Pupils should be able to:*	*Pupils could:*
LEVEL 1		
• follow directions, including the terms forwards and backwards, up and down, left and right, north, south, east and west	1a. follow directions	• follow routes using desk top and classroom plans
LEVEL 2		
• extract information from, and add it to, pictorial maps • draw around objects to make a plan, e.g. mathematical shapes, household objects • make representations of actual or imaginary places, e.g. their own bedroom, a treasure island • follow a route on a map, e.g. a map of the local area of the school • use pictures and photographs to identify features, e.g. homes, railways, rivers, hills and to find out about places	2a. use geographical vocabulary to talk about places 2b. make a representation of a real or an imaginary place 2c. follow a route using a plan 2d. identify familiar features on photographs and pictures	• make picture maps and plans • make their own 'treasure island' map • follow routes on their treasure island map • use air photographs to identify map features • organise a classroom score event
LEVEL 3		
• use the eight points of the compass • make a map of a short route, showing main features in the correct order, *e.g. from home to school* • locate their own position and identify features using a large scale map • identify features on oblique air photos	3b. use a large scale map to locate their own position and features outside the classroom 3c. make a map of a short route, showing features in the correct order 3d. identify features on air photographs	• use orienteering as a medium to show the importance of the compass directions • use the map of the school for orienteering exercises
LEVEL 4		
• use pictures and photographs to identify features, *e.g. homes, railways, rivers, hills* and to find out about places; describe what they see using geographical terms • interpret symbols, measure direction and distance, follow routes and describe the location of places using maps • make representations of real or imaginary places; make and use maps of routes, and sketch maps of small areas showing the main features and using symbols with keys • use the eight points of the compass • determine the straight line distance between two points on a map	4b. measure the straight line distance between two points on a plan 4f. draw a sketch map using symbols and a key	• measure distance taken on various routes • use a compass to reset the map • draw maps of apparatus inside as part of the school grounds
LEVEL 5		
• locate their position and identify features outside the classroom using a large scale map • identify features on vertical air photographs, e.g. railway lines, rivers and roads and match them to a map • use maps to find out where features are located and where activities take place	5a. interpret relief maps	• start learning about contours
LEVEL 6		
	6f. use map and compass to follow a route	• practise rough/fine bearings, aiming off • make a map

GEOGRAPHY AND ORIENTEERING IN THE NATIONAL CURRICULUM

▨ KNOWLEDGE AND UNDERSTANDING OF PLACES   ATTAINMENT TARGET 2 ▨

PROGRAMME OF STUDY	STATEMENT OF ATTAINMENT	EXAMPLES IN ORIENTEERING
Pupils should develop their awareness of localities in and beyond their own neighbourhood. Where possible such teaching should build on pupils' experience from visits, but should also use secondary sources, for example photographs, objects, stories, videos and accounts by teachers and other adults A locality should be a small area with distinctive features, e.g. the immediate vicinity of the school or of the pupil's home Pupils should be taught:	Pupils should be able to:	Pupils could:
	LEVEL 1	
	1a. name familiar features of the local area	• become familiar with the school map • look at maps of the local area
	LEVEL 3	
• to identify and describe landscape features in the local area, e.g. building, park, river, hill, valley, lake with which they are familiar	3c. use correct geographical vocabulary to identify types of landscape features and activities with which they are familiar in the local area	• use appropriate vocabulary to identify features on areas to be visited for orienteering

▨ ENVIRONMENTAL GEOGRAPHY   ATTAINMENT TARGET 5 ▨

PROGRAMME OF STUDY	STATEMENT OF ATTAINMENT	EXAMPLES IN ORIENTEERING
Pupils should be taught:	Pupils should be able to:	Pupils could:
	LEVEL 2	
• to identify activities which have changed the environment and consider ways in which they can improve their own environment	2b. describe ways in which people have changed the environment	• discuss if the school playground is a good environment for orienteering, a woodland sport? Could it be improved? Are we spoiling any part of the playground by orienteering?
	LEVEL 3	
• about activities intended to improve the local environment or a place they have visited	3a. describe effects on different environments of extracting natural resources	• describe some of the effects on landscape and wildlife caused by clearing woodland
	LEVEL 4	
• ways in which people look after and improve the environment; some of the ways in which damaged environments can be restored and damage prevented; and to consider whether some types of environment need special protection	4b. discuss whether some types of environment need special protection 4c. describe ways in which damaged landscapes can be restored	• discuss the problems of protecting special habitats of plants or wildlife where orienteers might run, such as wet marshland or rare woodland. Consider the positioning of control points

4   Lesson plans

INTRODUCTION

The following lessons enable the teacher to deliver attainment targets of the National Curriculum.

They also give a grounding in basic skills. Like most sports, orienteering has basic skills. These are:

Knowledge of map symbols
Orientating the map
Following handrails
Relocation
Route choice
Use of compass
Simplifying navigational problems

The fundamental skill in orienteering is orientating the map. The key to moving with a map is recognising the pattern of objects on the ground as the same as the pattern on the map and ALWAYS holding the map so that you are looking along the route to be followed.

Orientating the map is a thread which runs through all the lesson plans that follow.

INDEX OF LESSON PLANS

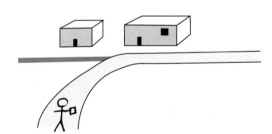

Orientate the map to correspond with the terrain

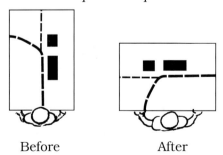

Before   After

The map can also be orientated with the help of a compass (see lesson 17).

LESSON 1

DESK TOP PLANS: SHAPES AND RELATIONSHIPS
IN THE CLASSROOM

NATIONAL CURRICULUM

Geography   Key Stage 1
Mathematics Key Stage 1

OBJECTIVES
- *To introduce the concept that maps and plans are a pattern of shapes*
- *To draw around objects to make a plan*
- *The use of words to describe position*
- *To develop understanding of the following terms:*
  SHAPES, PATTERN, PLAN, MATCHING

EQUIPMENT

Models of houses, trees and fences
Paper, pencils, coloured pencils/crayons
Coloured paper

Teacher preparation
Collect landscape models or objects with clear and contrasting shapes

Lesson
1. Place three objects on a sheet of paper in a very simple **pattern**. Draw round each piece then remove the objects to show the outline **shapes**. Discuss which shape **matches** which object and what shape each one is. A **plan** has been produced of the model.

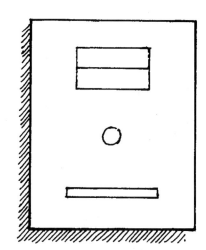

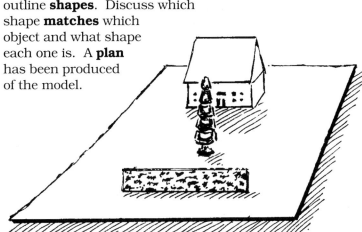

2. Place the objects in a different relationship. Draw the correct shapes on a piece of paper next to the model. Involve the children in deciding what shape to draw and where it should go. If the map is to be correct the drawing must match the model.

3. Give out paper and ask the children to draw the correct shapes in the right pattern. Place the objects on a central table, or use sets of objects with smaller groups of children.

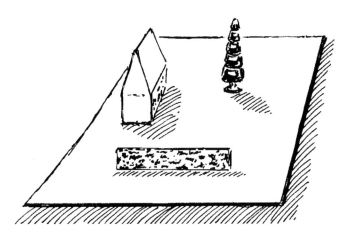

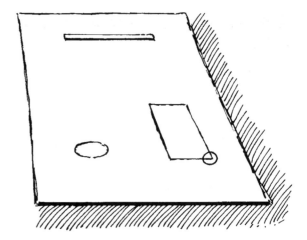

4. *Find the treasure*

Gather the class round the central table keeping the same pattern of objects, with each child having his/her own plan.

The children close their eyes while the teacher puts a cross or 'T' (for treasure) on the paper underneath part of one of the objects e.g. under the corner of a house. The teacher shows the class where the treasure is on the plan by marking on a red circle, then, pointing to the model, asks "Where is the treasure hidden?"

This should be repeated a few times. The **plan** must **match** the model if the treasure is to be found easily.

Next, let the children see where the treasure is to be hidden and ask them to mark on their plans where the treasure is to be found. This again can be repeated.

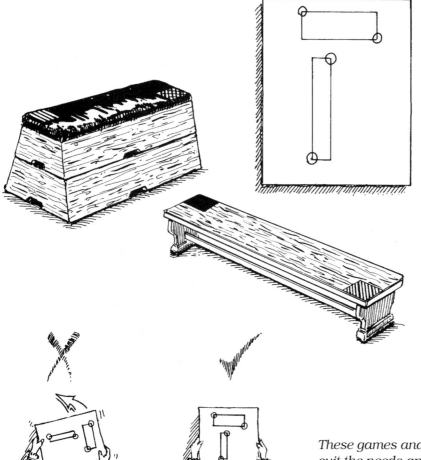

5. In a larger area, lay out two pieces of apparatus or furniture in a clear pattern. The children draw shapes to match. Some children may find this difficult.

Place a piece of coloured paper with 2-3 matching coloured crayons on one corner of each end of each piece of apparatus. Each child draws a circle on his/ her plan to indicate where the paper is. The children must **match** their plans to the apparatus (i.e. hold them the right way round) all the time.

6. Demonstrate that if you turn your plan a different way round the shapes do not match the apparatus. When the children have tried this for themselves, ask them to colour in the circles.

These games and exercises can be adapted to suit the needs and ability of your particular group of children. For example, the children of a class which understands these ideas quickly could practise walking towards a piece of apparatus from different parts of the area, keeping the plan set as they move.

22

USING TABLETOP PICTURE MAPS
IN THE CLASSROOM

NATIONAL CURRICULUM

Geography   Key Stage 1
Mathematics Key Stage 1

OBJECTIVES
- *To reinforce the concept that a map is like a picture*
- *To see how a map can be used to show, and help you follow, a route*
- *To locate positions on a map*
- *To follow directions*
- *To develop understanding of the following terms:*
  PICTURE MAP, SET, ROUTE, SYMBOLS, PLAN, DIRECTIONS

EQUIPMENT
Tabletop picture maps
Coloured pencils
Model houses and trees and a model car
String
Boards to lean on

Teacher preparation

Draw a simple picture map and a plan of a table top model or copy the ones shown on the next page.

Lesson

1. Set up the model to match the map. Give each child a copy of the picture map. The

2. Introduce the model car, which is going on a tour, visiting each of the houses. As the car is directed along its **route** the children follow where it goes on their picture maps, continually locating its position. Use the terms 'left' and 'right'.

3. Choose a new starting point. The children now draw in the route the car takes as it goes

children should stand or sit round 3 sides of the model so that they can relate their picture maps to the model. Ask them to **set** their maps and identify each of the houses and trees.

from house to house. A piece of string showing the route on the model will help them to draw the correct line. Arrows on the line will show the direction the car is going.

4. Give each child a **plan** of the model. Compare and match the picture map and the plan with each other and with the model. Identify the **symbols** showing trees and houses. **Set** the plan. Locate the start point of the route shown by the string and already drawn

on the picture maps.
Draw the route on to the plan by looking at the line of the string. Compare it with the line on the picture map.

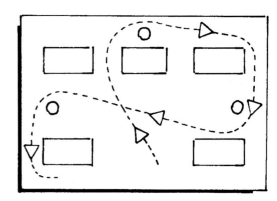

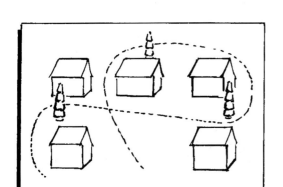

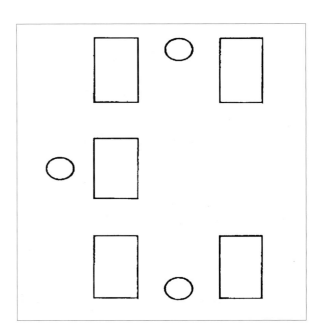

Summary

Maps are made up of **symbols**. Symbols are map language. The symbols can be read and seen as pictures of the features they represent. A map can be used to plan and follow a **route.**

Follow up

Children can make their own models and then make picture maps or plans of them. Plot in routes using string, and then transfer them onto the map.

The same lesson can be used to introduce the cardinal compass points, along with a globe and maps of the world. Use the compass to establish north. Place the model orientated to north. Label the model and the plans, marking north, south, east and west. Describe the location and direction of the features. Describe the routes according to directions taken.

Maps to copy

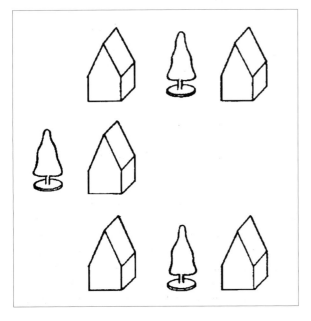

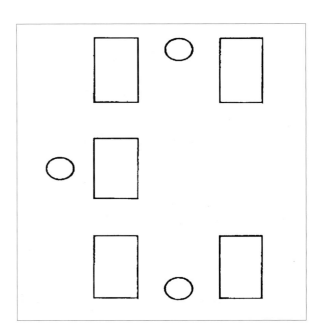

LESSON 3

A TREASURE ISLAND
IN THE CLASSROOM OR HALL

OBJECTIVES
- *To establish the meaning of the word "set" and follow up the use of shapes and symbols*
- *To extract information and add it to pictorial maps*
- *To make representation of imaginary places*
- *To follow a route and locate position*
- *To give instructions for movement along a route*
- *To develop understanding of the following terms:*
  MAP, SET, ROUTE

NATIONAL CURRICULUM

Geography Key Stage 1
Mathematics Key Stage 1

EQUIPMENT
Treasure island features, e.g. lake (water basin), river (blue rope or cord), house (box), trees (skittles or cones), field (outline with canes or rope), tracks (chalked lines) + paper, clipboards, crayons (blue, green, black, brown, red),

Teacher preparation
Collect equipment. Decide which area to use: younger children need to be able to overlook the whole area; older ones can use a larger area with bigger features. Read a story about an island.

Lesson
1. Give out paper, boards, crayons. Seat the children round the area to be used for the island.

2. Using chalk or rope, mark out the coastline of the island in a simple shape. As you add features on the island, the children draw them on their own paper. A mixture of pictures and symbols is quite acceptable for this map.

3. Place large features first: the lake (basin of water) and the river (blue cord) leading to it;

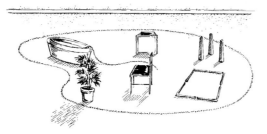

the box as the house; the cones (or pot plants) can represent trees; a chair can be a lookout tower. A field can be used to fill in the gaps.

4. **Story line**
Following a shipwreck a box of treasure is buried. Before being rescued the mariners make a **map** of the island so that the treasure can be found later. The children are the ship-wrecked mariners.

Ask the children where they want to bury their treasure. Mark the place with a "T".

Now years later you return to dig up your treasure and land on the island at the point where you are sitting. Mark it on your map with an arrow.

t = treasure

5. "Which **route** will you take to get to the treasure?" The teacher demonstrates. Plan the route looking at the model, then trace it on the map with a finger. The map must be kept **set** to follow the route.
A few children can talk through the route which they would follow, identifying the features they will pass by pointing at the model or the map.

6. If the island is big enough, the children can then try to follow the **route**, walking from one feature to the next until the treasure is reached.

7. Add north, south, east and west to the model and maps, then use those terms to describe positions and routes, e.g. Kay sits between the south and east ends of the island, the house is in the north.

Follow up
Talk about islands. Collect information about islands such as Australia, Britain or Iceland. Make maps of other areas or models.
This is an ideal starting point for cross-curricular work. Children can make their own imaginary island with features and treasure sites. Use this to talk about the island and make problems for friends to solve.

LESSON 4

ORIENTEERING STAR EXERCISE
IN THE PLAYGROUND OR SCHOOL FIELD

OBJECTIVES
- *To introduce orienteering*
- *To find features (controls) which are out of sight using a large scale map*
- *To locate positions*
- *To practise and improve performance*
- *To undertake simple orientation activity*
- *Decision making*
- *To develop understanding of the following terms:*
  ORIENTEERING, SET, CONTROL FLAGS

NATIONAL CURRICULUM

Geography   Key Stage 1
Mathematics Key Stage 1
Phys. Ed.   Key Stage 1

EQUIPMENT
Boards, size approximately 20 x 20 cm
Maps of the school and playground
8-10 mini-controls or coloured tapes
8-10 coloured wax crayons with string
Enlarged copy of map (approx A3) on board

Teacher preparation

Plan 8-10 control sites, some within sight and others just out of sight of the base/start. Mark the controls on all the maps, including the enlarged version, with red circles. (Use a circle template.) Number each circle. Tape the maps to the boards. Hang the control markers and crayons at the controls. Use the same start/base as for lesson 3.

Lesson

1. Give each child a map on a board. Go outside to the base shown as the triangle on the map. Set the map and discuss the features and symbols. The

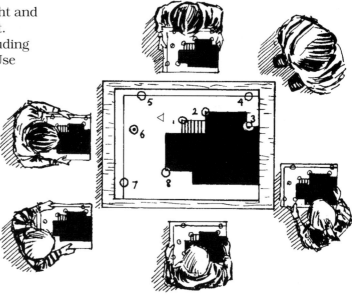

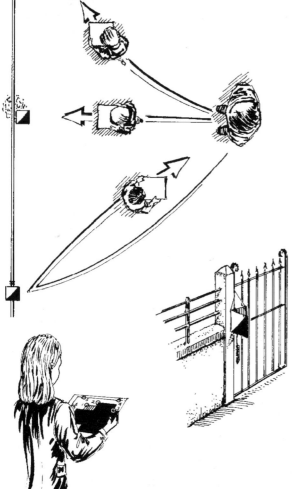

large A3 size map is useful for demonstrating how to set the map.

Identify (point out) a control. Set the map. Teacher and children run to the control. Repeat a few times, checking that everyone can set the map. Use a distinctive wall, hedge or road to help match the map to the ground. Point out the crayon hanging from the control.

2. Star exercise: each child is given one control to find. The child has to go to the control, colour in the right circle on the map with the crayon hanging there then return to base to join the queue ready for the teacher to identify the next control to visit.

Before running off the child should point out to the teacher the control flag he/she is going to, or, if it is out of sight, describe where it is.

Continue until most of the children have all the circles coloured in. Check that the colours are correct.

Further work

Some children could now go round the controls in a given order, marking control card boxes with the correct colour.

LESSON

5

POINT TO POINT ORIENTEERING
IN THE PLAYGROUND OR SCHOOL FIELD

OBJECTIVES
- *To remind the children that they should see the map as a picture*
- *To teach change of direction on the orientated map*
- *To practise orientation*
- *To practise locating their own position in relation to the landscape*
- *To recognise angles as a measurement of turn*
- *To develop understanding of the following terms:*
  KEEP THE MAP SET, ORIENTEERING, ROUTE, ORIENTATION

NATIONAL CURRICULUM

Geography	**Key Stage 1**
Mathematics	**Key Stage 1**
Phys. Ed.	**Key Stage 1**

EQUIPMENT
6-8 mini-control markers (or coloured tapes)
with wax crayons attached
A large (A3) map of the school and grounds
Small (A5) maps of the school and grounds
with control boxes down one edge

Teacher preparation

Plan 6-8 control sites. They should be mostly different from those used for lesson 4. Mark all the control sites on all the children's maps with red circles. Mark the start/finish with a triangle. Highlight a strip down one edge of the map with a bright colour. This need not necessarily be North, rather a hedge or wall which will act as the main reference line for setting the map. Hang the controls and crayons.

Lesson

1. In the classroom: Evaluate the group's understanding of the playground map and the symbols used. Look at the large map of the school and ask individual children to identify specific features e.g "Which entrance do you use to come into the school?"; "Which area is used for play at break time?" Ask them to close their eyes and imagine what each feature looks like: "Make a picture of it in your head". This is how they should 'read the map'.

2. Outside: Start at the triangle. Set the map using the coloured edge to help. Lay the map on the ground in front of you, still set.

On the map, find the control with number "1" beside it. This is the first control. Walk around the set map until you are looking in the direction of the control as viewed from the start. Pick up the map. The map is set. You are facing along the route you want to follow. DEMONSTRATE CLEARLY.

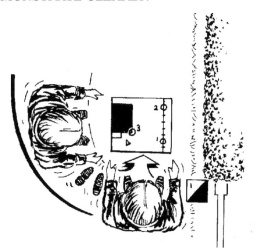

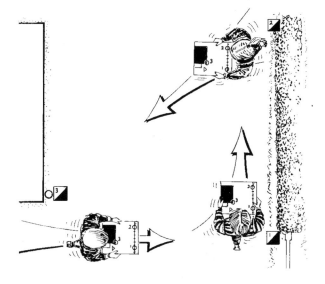

3. All go to control 1. Do not use the crayon. At each control follow this procedure:
- Set the map (on the ground, if this helps)
- Find the next control on the map. What is it?
- Walk around the map until you are facing the right way.
- Look. Can you see the marker? If not, plan your route.

Promote individual decision making.
- Make up your own mind about which way you should face.

Send the children round the course individually to practise this on their own. This time they should mark the control boxes with the coloured crayons. Start each child off as soon as the last has left the first control.

4. After each child has visited all the controls in the right order, send him/her round again. This time the circles on the map can be coloured in. The children needing extra help will have been identified by this time, and can be given more attention.

Further work

Draw symbols and write the name beside each
Show a video about orienteering
Find out when there will be a local event (see p.64 for addresses for information) and send information home to the parents to encourage the family to take part.

LESSON 6

LOOKING AT MAPS
IN THE CLASSROOM AND PLAYGROUND

NATIONAL CURRICULUM	
Geography	Key Stage 1
Phys. Ed.	Key Stage 1

OBJECTIVES
- *To use pictures and photographs to identify features*
- *To explore the potential for physical activity within the immediate environment*
- *To develop understanding of the following terms:*
  PLANS, MAPS, SYMBOLS, ROUTE, ORIENTEERING, CONTROL, RUNNING

EQUIPMENT
Local map including school + photocopies
10-15 mini/micro orienteering controls
Comprehensive selection of maps
Street plans, globe, world map, atlas
Adhesive, string, paper, pencils

Teacher preparation
Display maps. Place 10-15 controls.

General introduction
Children should be encouraged to bring in a wide variety of maps and a colourful wall display should be made. Try to use a collection of orienteering maps for one corner of the display - contact your local orienteering club for help.

Discuss the different map sizes, colours, why and how maps are used. Remind them about the idea of the map being an aerial or bird's-eye view of the ground. Each object or feature on the ground has a relationship with every other feature. This is reflected by the map. The map should be seen as a picture with all the features seen in the same relationship or pattern as those on the ground. The map can be pictured as a 3-dimensional model or miniature of the landscape, just like their tabletop maps.

Discuss the use of symbols on maps.

Use a road map to set tasks, e.g. finding the shortest route between towns.

Introduce the orienteering map. Explain the accuracy, detail and why it has been drawn, i.e. for a sport that involves running and map reading, called orienteering. Show the orienteering controls already used in the playground.

Practical
Playground game: the teacher puts out 10-15 controls, using adhesive or string, on prominent features, e.g. gate, football post, steps, etc. They should be between knee and head height. No map is used.

The children find as many controls as they can in a given time, e.g. 10 minutes. They carry paper and pencil and make a list of the code letters on each control.

If you have a map of the school, help the children to identify where the controls were found. Back in the classroom the letters could be used to make up words.

Physical Education
Use this opportunity to observe the changes to their bodies during 10 minutes running, e.g. becoming hot, breathing faster, sweating, heart beating faster, feeling tired, sore, thirsty.

ROUTE CHOICE
IN THE CLASSROOM AND PLAYGROUND

NATIONAL CURRICULUM

Geography	Key Stage 1 and 2
Phys. Ed.	Key Stage 1 and 2
Mathematics	Key Stage 1

OBJECTIVES
- *To build children's awareness and appreciation of maps through using them*
- *Decision making*
- *To develop understanding of the following terms:*
  ROUTE CHOICE, ORIENTEERING COURSE

EQUIPMENT
Local street map including school (one/child)
Playground maps premarked with lesson 6
  control sites
10-15 mini controls
Coloured cotton, chalk or crayons

Teacher preparation
Obtain maps. Place controls.

Classroom activity
Distribute local street maps and ask the
children to find the school, their own street,
the nearest train/bus station, a church, a
supermarket, etc. Have children draw in
features not already included, make a key if
necessary and colour in the map if suitable.

Tasks: children locate their homes and work
out the routes they take to school, and other
journeys.

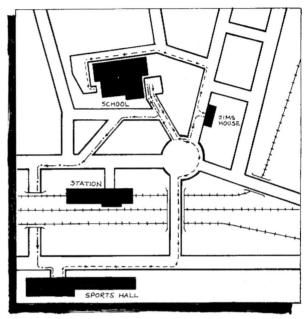

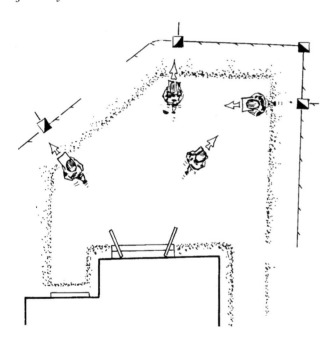

Emphasise route choice. Children work out
two or more routes between two places. Routes
can be shown in different colours using chalk,
crayons or cotton. The routes could be
discussed using an OHP.

Explain that in the sport of orienteering,
runners often have a choice of route when they
have to find control points on their course.

Practical
Distribute the playground maps with the
controls marked on from lesson 6.

In the classroom, the children decide as
individuals or as pairs in which order they will
find all the controls. They then go and find
them, copying each code letter onto their map.

The children then repeat this exercise, but
plan and visit the controls in a completely
different order. Remind them to always set the
map before going to next control.

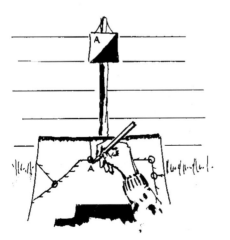

This exercise emphasises that the problems
presented can be solved in different ways. On
the second attempt, running can be encouraged

SCORE ORIENTEERING
IN THE CLASSROOM AND GYMNASIUM/HALL

NATIONAL CURRICULUM

Geography	Key Stage 1 and 2
Phys. Ed.	Key Stage 1 and 2
Mathematics	Key Stage 1

OBJECTIVES
- *To introduce score orienteering using a classroom map*
- *To locate features using a large scale map*
- *To use north to set the map*
- *To introduce rules in competition*
- *To develop understanding of the following terms:*
  CROSS COUNTRY, SCORE ORIENTEERING

EQUIPMENT
2 sets of matching cards (with different
   symbols drawn on)
Classroom maps
Mini controls
Adhesive (blu-tak), paper and pencils

Teacher preparation

Copy a good map of the classroom. Make one set of 10 cards with different symbols on each card and number them. Make an identical set of 10 cards but put letters on them.

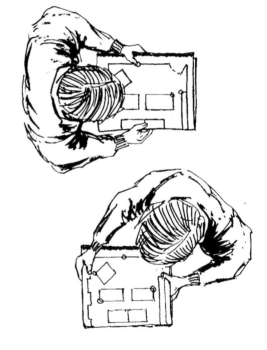

As each one is placed, the children mark the position on their maps with a clear circle in red and a number *beside* it, not in the middle. Do not allow the children to colour in the circles or triangle, otherwise the map detail will be hidden.

Teach map setting - make sure everything matches and *map north* is always to the *north end* of the classroom. Is it easier to set the map if you know where north is?

Classroom activity

Introduce the map of the classroom made by the teacher. Give one copy to each child.

Pupils mark their places with triangles. In orienteering the start is always shown by a triangle.

Mark the north edge of the map with a red crayon.

Place 10 lettered micro markers each on a different distinctive feature.

Ask the children to find each control, in any order, and mark the letter found on the control beside the appropriate circle on their map. They return to their seats when finished.

Give 10 points for each control (everyone should get 100 points). During the exercise check that the children:
(i) do not just spot the controls by looking around but read the map to decide where they are, and
(ii) keep the map set.

Explain *score orienteering* and show how it differs from *cross country orienteering* (*point to point orienteering* - lesson 5).

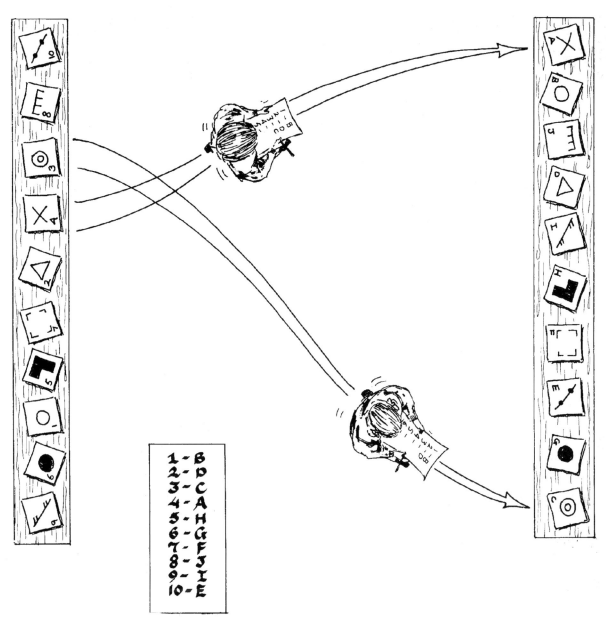

1 - B
2 - D
3 - C
4 - A
5 - H
6 - G
7 - F
8 - J
9 - I
10 - E

Practical in the gymnasium/hall

Lay out the matching sets of cards on benches, one set at each end of the gymnasium. The children write numbers 1-10 on a piece of paper. Give each child a number between 1 and 10. That is the card they start with.

The game is to run between the two benches matching the symbols and putting letters to numbers on the paper they are carrying.

Announce the rules:
- No touching the cards
- One number/letter at a time
- The winner is the one to get all the cards correct in the fastest time.

Increase the distance between the benches or play the game outside to increase the distance to run. Aim for about 5 minutes continuous

running. More than one set of cards may be needed. Half the class running at one time might be preferable.

Practical in pairs

Half the class plays the game while their partners watch, counting the number of times their partner runs back to the first bench.

Time how long it takes them to match all the numbers and letters

Partners sit down when one has finished. When all the first half has finished, repeat with the second half.

Start again, and see if they can perform faster the second time starting with a different number. Or write down the letters A-J and run to match the numbers.

Repetition here will contribute to more sustained exercise.

MAKING A MAP
IN THE GYMNASIUM/HALL

NATIONAL CURRICULUM	
Geography	Key Stage 1 and 2
Phys. Ed.	Key Stage 1 and 2
Mathematics	Key Stage 1

OBJECTIVES
- *To draw and then use a map of the gymnasium/hall*
- *To make a map with symbols and a key*
- *To introduce scale*
- *To develop understanding of the following terms:*
  MAPPING, SCALE, 'FOREST', PLOTTING

EQUIPMENT
Gymnastic apparatus, e.g. mats, benches,
  hoops, boxes, etc.
Rulers
Red marker
Paper and pencils

Teacher preparation
Plan the layout of the apparatus.
Draw a sample map.

Practical
(in the gym or a defined playground
area such as a netball court)
Each child has an A4 sheet of white
paper, pencil and ruler. Children
with learning difficulties should
be given a copy of the map
almost complete.

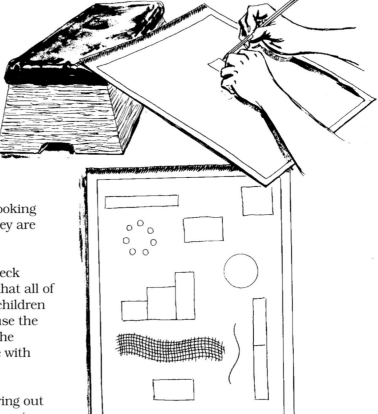

Ask the children to imagine they are looking
down on the area from the ceiling. They are
going to produce a map of the area.

Suggest the outline is drawn first. Check
when this has been completed to see that all of
the A4 sheet has been used. If some children
have drawn the four walls too small, use the
different sizes of outline to introduce the
concept of scale. Mark the north edge with
red.

Create a 'forest' in the gym/hall by laying out
a variety of gymnastic equipment, e.g. mats,
benches, hoops, table, badminton net
(descibed as a 'river'). Make sure the initial
'forest' is simple and keep the benches, boxes
and mats parallel to the walls.

Teach the children to plot the features onto
their maps starting with the most obvious

large feature in the centre. Then use
this as the basis for fixing the next
feature.

Using the apparatus laid out to make
a 'forest', take the children for a
'forest' walk. Suggest they keep the
map set as they walk through the
'forest'. The teacher should
demonstrate setting the map each
time direction is changed. The
children can then work in pairs,
taking it in turn to lead, running once
they can keep the map set.

Aim for 6-7 minutes running.

The map can be taken back to the
classroom, redrawn and coloured with
a key added.

LESSON

10

TREASURE HUNT
IN THE PLAYGROUND OR SCHOOL FIELD

NATIONAL CURRICULUM

Geography   Key Stage 1 and 2
Mathematics Key Stage 1

OBJECTIVES
* *To construct and use small maps of parts of the playground or field*
* *To establish the concept of pattern and relationship of one feature with another*
* *To develop understanding of the following terms:*
  TREASURE HUNT, MAP MAKING, DIRECTION

EQUIPMENT
'Treasure', e.g. class first names on pieces of card
'Big treasure', e.g. packet of sweets
Clipboards
Paper, pencils and crayons

Teacher preparation
Make name cards, place them in the playground. Make a sample map of the area to be used. Make cards for the location of the 'big treasure'.

Practical
Take the children outside to a suitable part of the playground or school field, containing very little other than a couple of buildings.

The children make a very simple map of this area. The emphasis, as in earlier mapping lessons, is on placing features in the right relationship to each other.

North, south, east and west (N, S, E, W) can be marked on the maps and used in discussion, e.g. the playing field is on the north side of the map.

When the map is completed, play 'treasure hunt'.

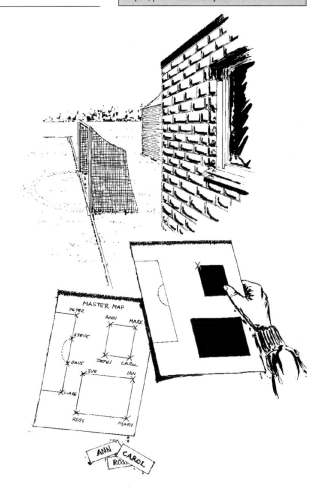

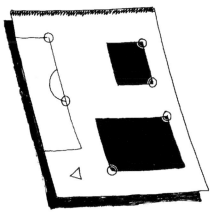

Treasure hunt
The teacher has placed a number of pieces of 'treasure' at distinct points within the area of the map.

The children locate one piece of treasure at a time. The teacher marks an X on each child's map which he/she uses to find the right treasure. They leave the treasure in place and report back what they have found.

The children change maps and find new treasure using a map with a different X on it. Collect in these treasures.

The teacher then puts out the 'big treasure' location cards in the same area.

The children visit the control sites in any order, write down all the words, then work out the message which indicates the location of the big treasure, e.g. a packet of sweets. They could work in pairs for this game.

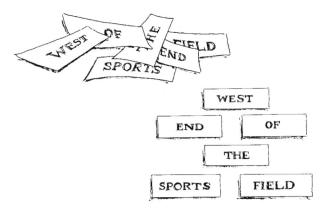

STAR EXERCISE
IN THE PLAYGROUND OR SCHOOL FIELD

LESSON **11**

OBJECTIVES
- *To introduce the new playground map*
- *To reinforce setting the map, orientation activity*
- *To help children maintain contact with the map as they move about*
- *To improve performance through practice*
- *To develop understanding of the following terms:*
  MAP CONTACT, SETTING THE MAP, STAR EXERCISE

NATIONAL CURRICULUM

Geography	Key Stage 1 and 2
Phys. Ed.	Key Stage 1 and 2
Mathematics	Key Stage 1

EQUIPMENT
Mini markers with numbers and code letters
Red crayons/pens
Playground maps
Pencils

Teacher preparation

This lesson is similar to lesson 4, using a map of a larger area, with controls further away from the base. Hang 8-10 mini markers on definite features in the playground or school field. Make a master map and plan a route to include all the controls.

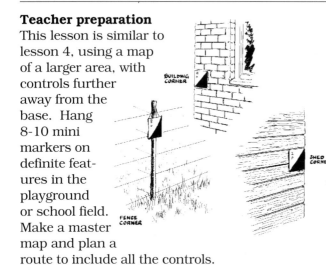

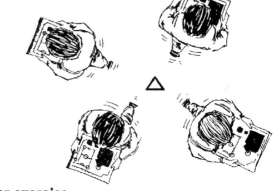

Practical

Using the playground map, take the class for a map walk. Each child must have his/her own map. Insist that the map is correctly set and that the children are able to point to their position on the map whenever they stop. NB Orienteers fold their maps and hold them with the thumb beside their last known position. This is part of keeping **map contact**.

During the walk, point out features and ask the children questions about map/terrain details. Ensure this is done slowly so that all children are always aware of their position on the map. The walk should lead past the mini markers which have been hung on definite features which are also on the map, e.g. 'fence corner' not just 'fence'.

At each marker the children draw a circle on their maps in the correct place. Check that they get this exactly right. Number the circles.

Star exercise

This is one of the best orienteering exercises for teaching skills to mixed ability groups. Individuals can work at their own pace and the teacher is in contact with the whole class.

Each child will return to the base (triangle) after finding each control.

Number the children to indicate which control each one is to find first, e.g. number 6 goes to control 6 first.

Emphasise to the children that they must return after each control, remembering the code letter. The teacher checks that they have memorised the correct letter.

Each time he/she returns to base, the map must be set with the child facing the right direction before going to the next control. The teacher can give help to those who need it.

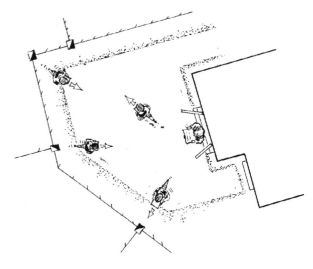

LESSON

12

SCORE ORIENTEERING COMPETITION
IN THE PLAYGROUND, SCHOOL FIELD OR LOCAL PARK

NATIONAL CURRICULUM
Geography   Key Stage 1 and 2
Phys. Ed.   Key Stage 1 and 2
Mathematics Key Stage 1 and 2
+ Social

OBJECTIVES
* *To complete the block of work with a class competition*
* *To promote individual decision making*
* *To develop understanding of the following terms:*
   MASTER MAP, SCORE EVENT, THINKING SEQUENCE

EQUIPMENT
10-15 mini markers with numbers and code
   letters
Master maps
Clock
Start banner

Teacher preparation
Set up a score event, hanging 10-15 mini markers on distinctive features marked on the map. Each marker should be visible (not hidden) so that the children can find them by reading the map. Draw up 4-5 master maps.

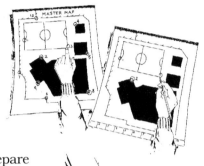

Classroom
The children prepare
for the score event by:
(1) drawing boxes in
spaces round the outside
edge of the front of the map
(not the back), so that the control codes can be copied when each control is found.
(2) copying the controls from a master map on to their own maps.
Teach them to point with a finger to a control on the master map when copying that control.

Practical
Set a time limit for the children to complete the course, e.g. 15 minutes. Explain that the purpose of the competition is to visit as many controls as possible within the time.

The controls can be visited in any order. Each control is worth a number of points (10 is the simplest) so they are trying to achieve as high a score as possible within the time. If they take longer they will have points deducted for each minute late. A very lenient penalty would be minus 5 per minute as it would probably take less than a minute to return from the farthest point of the playground.

Remind the children of the skills needed to find controls successfully:
(1) Keeping the map set.
(2) Always knowing where they are on the map.
(3) Remembering the thinking sequence . .
'Where am I? Where do I want to go? How do I get there?'

(4) Deciding in which order they want to find the controls (in this score event).

Hold a mass start (everyone starts together) and the children should complete the score event within the time limit. Each child can add up his/her own score. With nearly all the children gaining maximum scores, the competitive element can be played down. Discussion can take place on route choice. Promote an atmosphere of enjoyment in completing the course to the best of your ability (not simply to beat someone else).

Children who ask if they can do more orienteering could be given an information sheet including the name and address of the local club secretary and the dates of the next local events.

Microcomputing and orienteering
Does your school have a microcomputer? Software exists that may enable you to link what your children have been learning in their orienteering programme to the computer. Take advantage of this opportunity to allow your class to familiarise themselves with the scope of the computer by playing educational games currently available and suitable for primary use.

LESSON
13
LINE ORIENTEERING
IN THE GYMNASIUM/HALL

NATIONAL CURRICULUM

Geography	Key Stage 2
Phys. Ed.	Key Stage 2

EQUIPMENT
Gym apparatus
Maps
Pencils or crayons
Mini maps for each team of 3-4

OBJECTIVES
- *To revise map to ground observation*
- *Running and team activity*
- *To develop understanding of the following terms:*
  LINE ORIENTEERING, MINI MAPS, TEAM

Teacher preparation

Lay out a simple pattern of apparatus. Draw a plan and copy for each pupil, or ask the pupils to draw in the shapes themselves. Mark the north side with a colour.

Practical

Each pupil creates a line which shows an interesting route weaving around (or under or over) the apparatus. Draw the line and follow it round. Hold the map with two hands out in front and let it 'steer' you around. Keep it set all the time. Use the north side of the area to set the map. Swop maps and follow someone else's line.

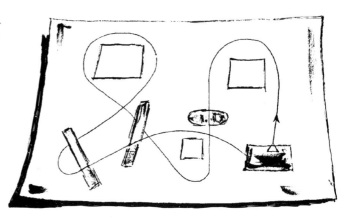

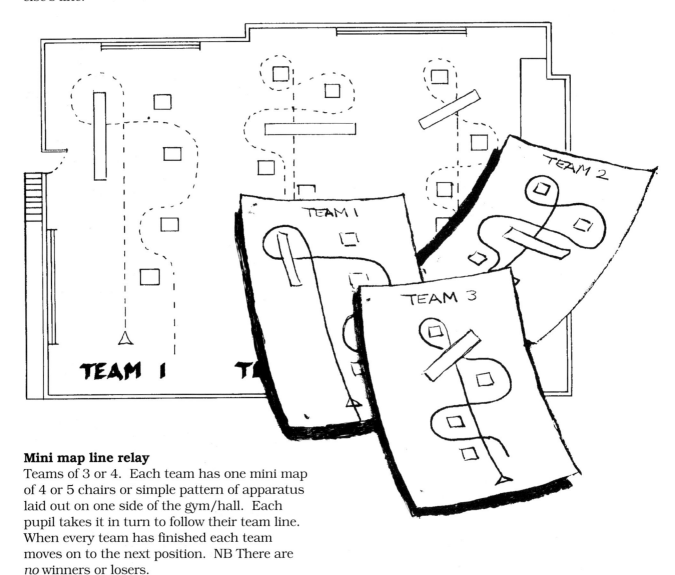

Mini map line relay

Teams of 3 or 4. Each team has one mini map of 4 or 5 chairs or simple pattern of apparatus laid out on one side of the gym/hall. Each pupil takes it in turn to follow their team line. When every team has finished each team moves on to the next position. NB There are *no* winners or losers.

14

LINE ORIENTEERING
IN PARK OR WOODLAND

OBJECTIVES
- *To encourage continuous map contact*
- *Thumbing the map*
- *Individual decision making*
- *Sustained running activity*
- *To specify locations and movement from angles on the map and route*
- *To develop understanding of the following terms:*
  THUMBING, CONCENTRATION, MAP CONTACT

NATIONAL CURRICULUM
Geography   Key Stage 2
Phys. Ed.   Key Stage 2
Mathematics Key Stage 2
+ Environmental Education

EQUIPMENT
Pencils (on string)
Maps
Controls

Teacher Preparation

Plan a circular route following line features (mainly paths) with lots of changes of direction. This should be about 800m long, not more because of the level of concentration required to follow it. Put out 3-6 control markers at distinctive points along the route. The first control

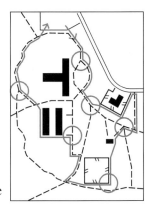

should be near the beginning of the line. Mark up the maps with a red line showing the route the children have to follow. Do not mark the controls on the map. Children find this type of exercise quite hard because they are used to running freely until they see the flag. In this exercise they have to read the map all the time. *Assistant:* Puts out controls. Helps children to follow the line.

Lesson

1. Use a short map walk to familiarise the group with the map and surrounding terrain. Revise setting the map. Explain the purpose of the lesson. Each pupil will follow the route

shown by the red line on the map. If the route is followed correctly they will find control flags and can then mark the position of each control on the map. Show how to hold the map and trace progress with the thumb (thumbing).

2. Thumb the start and take the whole group along the line to the first control. Mark the position of this control accurately on the maps. Use language associated with angles when appropriate.

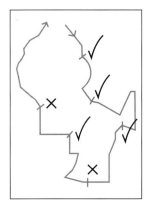

3. Allow the more able to continue on their own to the next control. If they mark that correctly then let them continue round to the finish and wait there. Continue behind with the remainder of the group sending them ahead as they become more competent and their confidence increases.

4. Check the maps to see if the controls have been marked accurately. Some may have made mistakes.

5. Go round the route again with the whole group together. Check that the children are in contact with the map at each control marker. Practise looking at the map as you walk or run along. Thumbing the map helps to do this quickly.

6. Before collecting the markers have a running race round the same route.

"The best orienteers read the map whilst they are running; they are very fit and know where they are all the time".

LESSON

15

ROUTE CHOICE (+ HANDRAILS, MAP COPYING)

IN PARK OR WOODLAND

OBJECTIVES
- *To emphasise the importance of choosing a route*
- *To show the advantages of using line features as handrails*
- *To understand scale and distance*
- *The use of networks to solve problems*
- *Decision making*
- *Environmental awareness*
- *To develop understanding of the following terms:*
  HANDRAILS, ROUTE CHOICE, LINE FEATURES, SCALE

NATIONAL CURRICULUM
Geography   Key Stage 2 and 3
Phys. Ed.   Key Stage 2
Mathematics Key Stage 2
+ Environmental & Social Education

EQUIPMENT
Maps and route choice card game
Control markers and codes
Control cards and punches/crayons
Pens
Safety pins

Teacher Preparation

Collect a variety of maps and make up cards with one route choice problem on each card. Cover the cards with transparent film. Each route should include 2-4 different line features linking each pair of controls. Number the cards, and include scale and legend on the back.

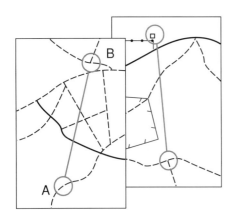

Route choice card game

Select an area where you could set up a star exercise with 2-3 features linking the base to each control. Make three Master Maps showing all controls and the Base/Start. Include a list of control descriptions. Put the start on each map. Controls should be within 250 metres.

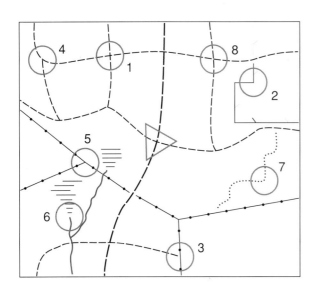

Safety: star exercises take place in a safe contained area with straightforward group management. Ensure the children understand that they must return to base after finding each control.

Assistant: Puts out controls - each having a code letter, and a punch or coloured crayon.

Lesson

1. Use the card game for a school-based lesson to discuss route choice, handrails and scale.

2. In the park or woodland give out control cards. Each pupil pins one to his/her clothing.

3. Explain how the star exercise works. Each participant must return to the start after finding each control. Give each child a number. This is the number of the control that child is to copy and find first. Two or three children at a time copy one control each onto their maps. The teacher checks for accuracy. Each pupil describes the route he/she will take before setting off. A NORTH arrow on the ground will facilitate map setting.

4. As each pupil returns, check the punch mark, then ask the child to copy the next control and its description from the Master Map. Aim for each pupil to visit 3 - 5 controls.

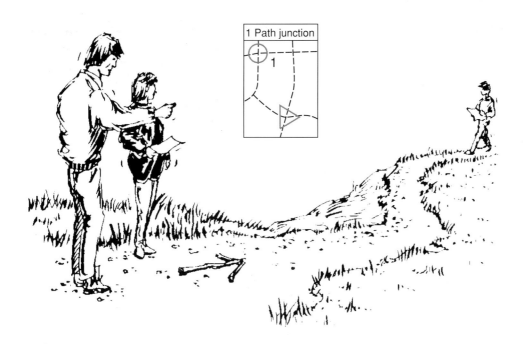

5. At the end have a competition to see who can bring in the controls the fastest: one pair of children per control. They could go out together and return by separate routes. Calculate which was the fastest pair. Eg. Gary & Angela No 2 250m in 2mins 30secs = 10 minutes per kilometre.

Scale and distance measurement
Use these controls to discuss scale. Measure the distance taken to each control and work out how far it is:

Map 1:5,000: 1millimetre (mm) = 5 metres (m)
so distance to Control 1 = 20mm = 100m

Map 1:10,000: 1mm = 10 metres
so distance to control 1 = 20mm = 200m

INTRODUCING THE COMPASS
IN THE CLASSROOM

NATIONAL CURRICULUM
Geography   Key Stage 2 and 3
Phys. Ed.   Key Stage 2
Mathematics Key Stage 2
+ Environmental & Social Education

EQUIPMENT
Examples of a map guide compass, a protractor compass and a thumb compass
Set of compasses (one for each pupil)
Direction cards

OBJECTIVES
- *To introduce the compass as an aid to navigation*
- *To understand and use bearings to define directions*
- *To develop understanding of the following terms:*
  MAP NORTH, MAGNETIC NORTH, COMPASS NORTH, PARALLEL

Teacher preparation
Display the three types of compass (see page 43) and a large labelled diagram. Make up a set of cards with the eight cardinal directions marked.

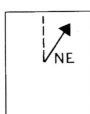  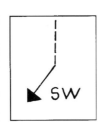

Direction cards

Lesson
1. Show the three types of compass to the class.
2. Distribute a set of compasses. Examine the compasses and discuss the parts.
3. The pupils draw a compass and label it.
4. Design and draw a compass rose showing the eight cardinal points.

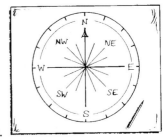

5. Use the compass to find Magnetic North in the room, then determine each of the other cardinal points. Include language associated with angles.
6. Each child draws a plan of his/her desk and uses the compass to mark North-South lines on the plan. Draw several parallel lines indicating map north.

7. Allow further opportunities for establishing the cardinal directions within the classroom.
8. Move to a hall or larger area and use the set of direction cards. Ensure each child has a card. Indicate which side of the area is North. The children run round swopping cards at frequent intervals, when the whistle goes each pupil runs to the corner or side indicated on the card. Show them how to set the card to North to find the correct direction.

17

SETTING THE MAP USING A COMPASS
IN SCHOOL GROUNDS OR PARKLAND

NATIONAL CURRICULUM
Geography   Key Stage 2 and 3
Phys. Ed.   Key Stage 2 and 3
Mathematics Key Stage 2 and 3
+ Environmental Education

OBJECTIVES
- *To establish that map north and magnetic (compass) north must always match on an orientated map*
- *To practise orienteering using a map and compass*
- *To develop understanding of the following terms:*
  COMPASS, MAP NORTH, MAGNETIC NORTH, COMPASS NORTH

EQUIPMENT
Compasses
Maps
Control cards and pins
Control markers, codes, punches/crayons

Teacher preparation

In a familiar area, prepare a mini-course star exercise with several controls which can be linked from different directions. Make a master map with all the controls on. Mark the pupils' maps with the start and two controls for the group practice.
Assistant: Puts out controls, helps at the Start/Base

Lesson

1. Pin on the control cards then hand out the maps and compasses. If using the map guide compass, show how to clip it to the side of the map.
Go through the teaching stages given on the next page, then show the group how to set the map with the compass.
2. With the whole group together, visit the two controls on the maps using the compass to set the map at each control. Return to the start.
3. Explain the star exercise. The pupils line up and are given two or three new controls to visit. Mark different mini courses on each pupil's map. Check that the map is set before the child sets off. Assistance is essential with a group of eight or more.

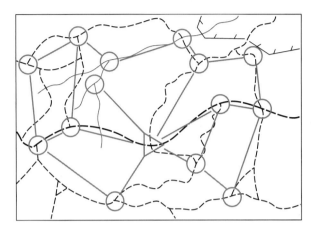

4. Use the last 15 minutes to bring in the control markers.
5. Pupils work out how far they have been during the lesson, eg. 2.5 km in 50 minutes.

Follow up
A variety of compass exercises in the school grounds.

Teaching stages

1. Establish NORTH. The magnetic needle always points North-South. Wherever you face, however you twist or turn, the compass needle always points to north.

2. Fold the map square and small enough to 'thumb' your location. Hold the map so that you are looking straight along the route you want to take.

MAP GUIDE

THUMB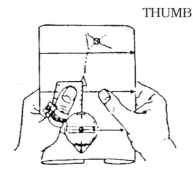

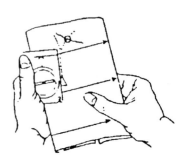

PROTRACTOR

3a. MAPGUIDE. Hold the map steady using two hands to 'steer'.

3b. THUMB. Place your thumb and the corner of the leading edge at your location. Use the other hand to help hold the map steady at first.

3c. PROTRACTOR. Place the edge of the compass alongside the route you want to take. Use two hands to hold the map steady at first.

4. Turn yourself with map and compass fixed in front of you until the magnetic needle lies parallel to North-South lines on the map. Needle North = Map North.

5. You are now facing along the direction line you want to take. Take the spare hand away from the map: off you go! The protractor compass can be held in the opposite hand to the map if preferred.

PROTRACTOR

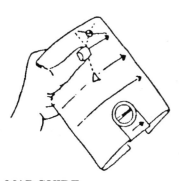

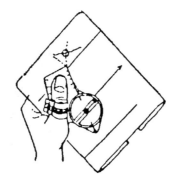

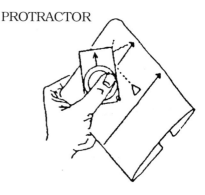

MAP GUIDE

THUMB

6. Continue to read the map with your thumb. When the path changes direction - move your thumb - turn the map to look straight along the line you want to take - check that the Needle North points to Map North

Points to watch
Always keep map and compass horizontal to allow the needle to swing freely.
Hold map and compass about waist level.
Lots of practice with accurate feedback is essential for understanding.

Orienteering compasses

The compass is a direction finding instrument invaluable as an aid to precise navigation. Correct use will allow the orienteer to keep the map orientated in order to select routes and follow them faster while maintaining contact with the map. Maps used for orienteering have only magnetic North lines. This enables the compass to be used easily for map orientation.

Orienteers use three different types of compass. The map guide or clip compass (Fig 1), the protractor compass (Fig 2) or the thumb compass (Fig 3).

Map guide compass
This is designed and recommended to help the beginner to concentrate on looking at and thumbing the map, once it is orientated.

Protractor compass
The protractor compass can be used to take bearings as well as set the map. It requires careful teaching and considerable practice to use this compass accurately.

Thumb compass
This is ideal for older beginners but can be an encumbrance for children: their small hands are needed primarily to hold the map. The single unit (map and compass) helps to focus attention on the map.

It is important that whichever compass is chosen it is used in the correct way.

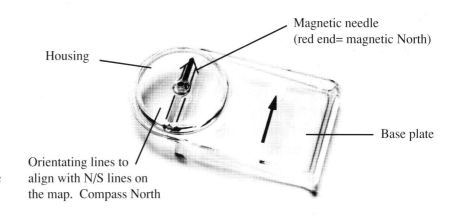

Housing

Magnetic needle
(red end= magnetic North)

Base plate

Orientating lines to align with N/S lines on the map. Compass North

Map Guide Compass

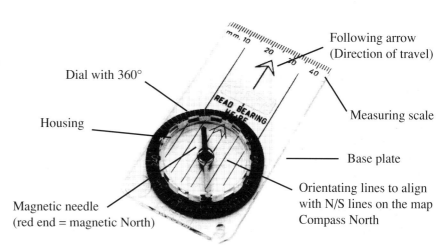

Dial with 360°

Housing

Magnetic needle
(red end = magnetic North)

Following arrow
(Direction of travel)

Measuring scale

Base plate

Orientating lines to align with N/S lines on the map Compass North

Protractor Compass

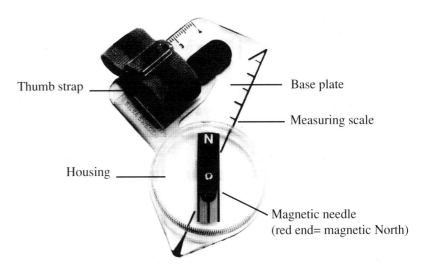

Thumb strap

Housing

Base plate

Measuring scale

Magnetic needle
(red end= magnetic North)

Thumb Compass

LESSON 18

NAVIGATING BY CONTOURS
IN AN AREA WITH GOOD CONTOUR DETAIL

NATIONAL CURRICULUM
Geography   Key Stage 2 and 3
Phys. Ed.   Key Stage 2 and 3
Mathematics Key Stage 2 and 3
+ Environmental Education

OBJECTIVES
- *To introduce contours as an additional aid to good navigation*
- *To interpret relief*
- *Two dimensional representation of three dimensional objects*
- *To develop understanding of the following terms:*
  CONTOUR LINES, STEEPNESS, SHAPE, UPHILL, DOWNHILL

EQUIPMENT
Maps
Control markers

Teacher Preparation

Give a short introduction to contours in the classroom. Follow with a visit to an area with distinctive contour features. Plan a map walk and a short course (0.5-1km) with control points on contour features. Make up control description lists using contour terms, eg. hill top, foot of steep slope, re-entrant, spur. Pupils will only be able to complete a course on their own if they have already developed confidence in map reading.

Assistant: Patrols the course area and assists with map walk.

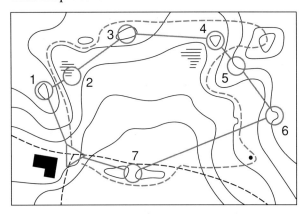

Lesson

1. Map walk: lead the group showing examples of shape and slope.
2. Demonstrate and practice how to set the map by looking at the shape of ground. Navigate to features by using the contours.
3. Go to the start of the course. Set pupils off at intervals. The controls should be quite close together so that the contour feature is distinctive and simple, e.g. 1-2: Down the hill to the bottom.

2-3: The second hilltop along.

3-4: A hill on its own in a flat area.

Have a safety direction and an assistant patrolling the area or helping at the control sites.

4. The children mark up their routes and describe the contour features they used to reach the controls.

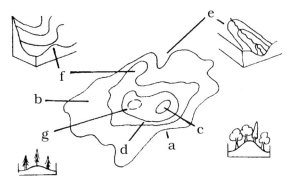

a: Contours close together show steep ground.
b: Contours spaced apart show a gradual slope or flatter ground.
c: A ring contour shows a hill top.
d: The more contours there are, the higher the hill.
e: A valley or re-entrant is shown by a bend in a contour pointing to the uphill side. It may or may not have a stream in it.
f: A spur or ridge is shown by a nose-shaped contour line.
g: A form line (intermediate contour) helps to improve the picture the map gives to the orienteer.

Follow up

Make contour models at school. Use a contour card game.

PREPARATION FOR FINAL COMPETITION
IN THE CLASSROOM

NATIONAL CURRICULUM

Geography	**Key Stage 2 and 3**
Phys. Ed.	**Key Stage 2 and 3**

OBJECTIVES
- *To familiarise everyone with the park/woodland map to be used in lesson 20*
- *To give information on local events and the local orienteering club*
- *To provide an opportunity for social education, fair competition, environmental awareness*
- *To develop understanding of the following terms:*
  CONTOURS, ORIENTEERING CLUB, BADGES

EQUIPMENT
Park/woodland maps covered with
  adhesive film
Photocopies of the same map
Local club handout and fixture list
Spirit-based red pens (fine tip)

Preparation

Cover coloured maps with adhesive film. Plan 1 or 2 courses for lesson 20; one can be slightly longer but both must be really easy because of the unfamiliar terrain, eg. 1.0 - 1.5km with 8 - 12 controls. All controls should be linked by only one line feature on each leg. In open parkland each control should be visible from the previous one.

Permanent courses: if a permanent course is to be used, prepare the maps in the same way. The pupils can then link the controls to be visited with a red line.

Assistance: arrange for parents or other adults to assist (do not presume that they can read a map). Attendance at this preparation lesson would be useful.

Lesson

- Give a copy of the coloured map to each pupil, plus a photocopy. The coloured maps can be used many times if they are covered with clear adhesive film and a permanent felt tip used to draw in circles and routes. Banda fluid or methylated spirit will remove felt tip marks easily.

- Practise copying the course from a Master Map on to the coloured map unless it is already pre-marked.

- Route description exercises - verbal or written

- CONTOURS - if there are any on the map, discuss their purpose. They won't be seen on the ground! and they can't be followed like a track!

- Key - look for examples of the different symbols with an emphasis on line features and colours. Play a game or organise a quiz to improve familiarity with the key.

Discuss

The plan for next lesson:
Outing to the park/woodland.
Equipment and clothing.
Food?
Criteria for the starting order.

Rules and safety:
Use of whistle only in emergency.
Everyone MUST REPORT TO THE FINISH.
No shouting or calling.
No litter.
Controls must be found in the right order.

How to carry on orienteering - local club.
Events always open to beginners (handout).

Fixtures
Colour-coded courses are most common. Progress through the colours which increase in difficulty. White - Yellow - Orange - Red - Green - Blue - Brown. The course for lesson 20 will be of white or yellow standard. Some events you enter according to your age and sex eg. M10 or W10 for boys and girls aged 10 years or under.

Fixture lists can be obtained from your local club or regional fixtures secretary through the British Orienteering Federation.

Badge schemes
Some regions have their own badge schemes to encourage participation. e.g. Scotland - a badge when 5, 10 and 20 events have been completed. The colour-coded badge scheme is administered by local clubs. To gain a colour badge you must finish 3 courses of the same colour in the top half of those who started or within one and a half times the winner's time. Pairs can also qualify for colour awards.

Keep the coloured maps but let the children take the photocopy home to look at.

LESSON 20

FINAL COMPETITION
IN LOCAL PARK OR WOODLAND

OBJECTIVES
- *To give a taste of real orienteering*
- *To complete the series of lessons*
- *To provide opportunities for cross curricular work - environmental education, social education, design technology, language*
- *To develop understanding of the following terms:*
  LINE FEATURES, ROUTE CHOICE, MAP COLOURS, CROSS COUNTRY EVENT

NATIONAL CURRICULUM
Geography   Key Stage 2 and 3
Phys. Ed.   Key Stage 2 and 3
Mathematics Key Stage 2 and 3
Cross curricular

EQUIPMENT
Premarked maps, description and code lists
Control cards, safety pins, pencils
Full size control markers + punches/crayons
Tapes for marking walk, clock, compasses
Compasses, whistles, waterproofs

1 MAP WALK. This is essential before starting the competition. Take the group for a map walk following a pre-marked route. Point out features and revise map setting. Look at contours if they are on the map. Indicate changes of vegetation (colour). Highlight the line features they will have to follow on the course. Use the sun in the south to set the map. The map walk should finish at the START area for the competition.

2 Give a start order and times. Encourage individual participation and a positive attitude. Emphasise that they should do their best to find all the controls.

3 Before starting, pin control card and descriptions to clothing. Start time to be written on the card.

4 Using a one-minute start interval set them off. If there are two courses, two can start at once. CROSS COUNTRY COURSE 1.0km - 1.5km, estimated time will be 12 - 30 minutes.

5 FINISH. Set up a timing system at the same time as the start. Put any spare staff or parents out at one or two controls, suggest that they only offer advice if asked for or if the pupil is obviously going the wrong way.

6 RESULTS. Calculate results and display. Praise all those who found all the controls. Add time on for each control missed rather than disqualify. Early finishers can help with the results. A plan should be made beforehand to cope with the possibility of someone getting lost. They should be told to stay on a track or path somewhere in the area.

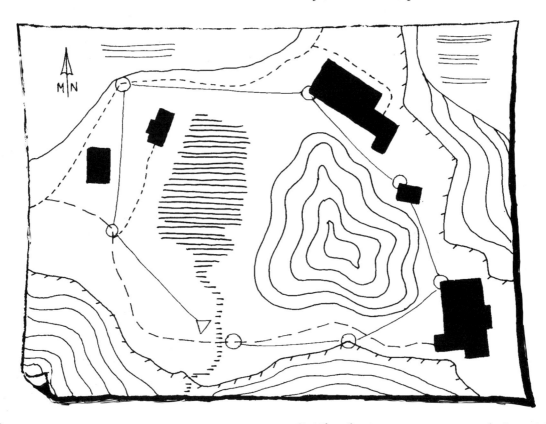

Safety
Consideration of the area and the amount of help available will influence how independent the pupils can be. Make sure everyone knows where the base is (e.g. car park) and that they should return there when they finish.

Getting lost - emergency signal. In outdoor adventurous activities the emergency signal for someone completely lost or injured and requiring help is 6 long blasts on the whistle repeated at one minute intervals. The response by the searcher is 3 short blasts.

5   Assessing orienteering activities within the National Curriculum

The teaching and learning of orienteering cannot be separated from assessment. It is an important and inter-related part of the process and should not be regarded as an 'add-on' activity. Assessment has two essential purposes. First, it should tell us about individual progress, i.e. what a particular child has learned and achieved. Second, it should assist the teacher in evaluating the teaching methods, content and organisation, and provide a basis for forward planning.

There is also a third element. Assessment is diminished if the results are not communicated. Knowing how the young orienteer has performed not only allows accurate feedback and positive reinforcement to be given but also puts the teacher in a position to inform other interested parties. We all need to know how we are doing and how improvements can be made. Assessment aids this process.

Assessment should be continuous and conducted during the teaching activities. It should be concerned with what a child knows and can do, seen against a Statement of Attainment (SoA).

THE INFORM PROCESS

The Schools Examination and Assessment Council (SEAC) have produced a six step process of teacher assessment called INFORM. Though printed below as a list the process should be seen in the round. There is no first or last step.

Identify Statements of Attainment your lesson plans will promote

Note carefully opportunities for the child to demonstrate attainment

Focus on the performance, looking for evidence of attainment

Offer the child the chance to discuss what has been achieved

Record what you have identified as noteworthy

Modify future lesson plans for the child accordingly

It seems straightforward, but is it? Let us look at two examples of how the INFORM process can be applied to the topic of orienteering.

EXAMPLE 1

Attainment Target 1 : Geographical Skills Statement of Attainment Level 2C "Follow a route using a plan" [AT1 Geography 2C]

Content: The content relates to many of the progressive activities set out in the lessons in Chapter 4, and in particular to numbers 2, 3, 4, 5, 7, 11, 13, 14 and 15.

Context: The teaching has been arranged to equip the young orienteer to follow a route or a trail around the school playground or site using a map which might have been produced by the teacher, another adult or a child. The children are now ready to be tested.

The assessment task raises three questions for the teacher:

Q.1. Is the task relevant to a particular SoA?

Q.2. Is the response of the child appropriate to the SoA?

Q.3. How many times should the child demonstrate the attainment of this kind of activity?

It is clear that the answer to question one is Yes. But how do we judge a child's response? The key is to make systematic observations of an individual. It may mean that on this occasion other children are not monitored. Equally, the children could be assessed in turn.

There is also a need to be clear about the evidence to be gathered. What constitutes a successful response? The criteria need to be agreed beforehand. For example, is it acceptable for the child to complete the task if he took one wrong turn at a junction but then corrected himself? Is it acceptable if the child completed the route but did not maintain contact with the map by using a thumbing technique?

	Experience outdoor and adventurous activities that involve navigation
	Be taught the skills necessary for the activity undertaken
AT1 Eng 3a	Relate a real event in a connected narrative which conveys meaning to a group of pupils
AT1 Eng 4a	Give a detailed oral account of an event .... explain with reasons why a particular course of action was taken.

There are multiple SoA in four curricular areas to attend to here. The SoA do serve as measures against which learning can be judged and they do indicate what evidence to look for to see if achievement matches the target. However, the problem is where to focus. The tasks are conducted in a sequence and in theory it should be possible, but the reality may be problematic. The advantage is that several attainment targets are being addressed within a meaningful context.

A variety of different forms of evidence is being generated.

- *symbolic* ... control sites, start and finish

- *written/symbolic* ... control description sheet

- *practical* ... correct location of controls

- *practical* ... completion of course

- *oral* ... discussion of results

- *oral* ... comparison of performance

Overload can be the problem but the key to assessment is the clear understanding which the teacher will have of the structure of the SoAs underlying the individual children's response to the task.

Recording can then be made against the individual's name in each of the subject areas. The advantage is that multiple targets have been assessed in one task. The disadvantage is that considerable recording is necessary.

The assessment described above is formative (ongoing) and serves diagnostic, evaluative and information purposes. Eventually we reach the point when the overall achievement of the child has to be assessed. This takes place at the end of a Key Stage and is referred to as summative assessment.

On the following pages we show how the topic of orienteering fits into the four subject areas of Geography, Mathematics, English and PE. Each Statement of Attainment relevant to an orienteering activity has been placed within a level and the code letters adhered to, so that results from this topic can be transferred to the school's records. The boxes prefacing each statement can be used for recording purposes. Colour coding can be used or a simple symbol system devised to show that the SoA is achieved or that the target was visited and experienced but not attained.

Finally, what problems might you encounter in assessment?

First let us be aware that children's performance does differ from day to day so we must be careful to interpret the evidence. If the topic, skill, or activity does not show confident attainment then a repeated assessment may be necessary.

Second, as assessors we need to be clear about what is being assessed and what constitutes the necessary evidence to state that an SoA has been achieved. It is important to discuss this with colleagues and reach agreement as to what constitutes success.

As the young orienteers become more confident the nature of the tasks they tackle grows in complexity and may require them to work collaboratively, eg completing a team score event, or planning an activity for others.

Assessing collaborative effort is difficult. An overview can be taken but individual efforts within the activity will need to be noted. We should ask ourselves "What are the positive contributions of this child at this moment?" and "How are they perceived by the group?"

Records need to be kept but equally, balances have to be struck regarding the amount of detail and frequency of the assessment and the evidence to be gathered to allow the summative (end stage) assessment to be made.

Assessment is complex, and since orienteering is not a subject within the National Curriculum but a potential vehicle for cross curricular activity, the assessment, and subsequent recording and reporting, may be daunting.

But many of the activities will be practical skills, observable and open to discussion. As such they can be assessed. The teacher who understands the inter-relatedness of the appropriate SoAs will possess a clarity which will enable judgements to be made. If the discussion of the activities is shared with the participants and other teachers then reliable and valid judgements can be made which will benefit the teaching and further the progress of the children.

The incident of the wrong turn, though corrected, might mean that you require the child to demonstrate competence in a new situation. With regard to not keeping map contact, though we as orienteers know this is a desirable technique, it is not necessary for the SoA. The evidence is that the child followed the correct path thus achieving the objective. Both situations raise the question as to how much evidence should be gathered and whether this should be in more than one situation.

Regardless of the outcome it is important to record how the child performed and use the information as a reference point for future tests. The careful observation of how the child carried out the task, i.e. not keeping map contact, can also be used to decided when this technique should be introduced.

In order to interpret the evidence correctly it is helpful to give the child the chance to discuss what happened. You can put questions such as "I saw you make a mistake at the path junction but you corrected yourself. How did you do that?" or "I see you completed the route successfully but you hardly seemed to keep track of where you where. How did you do it so well?" The teacher helps the child by describing what he did and can confirm the progress made or explain how help can be given.

In this example the evidence was gained by systematic observation of one pupil at a time against an agreed criteria. The progress of the child can be recorded and if repeated in novel situations, can be seen to match the Statement of Attainment.

Now let us consider an alternative example. In this situation the teacher has conducted an activity and dwells on the children's response. The activity is cross curricular and more demanding than example one.

EXAMPLE 2

This exercise relates to lessons 5, 10 and 15 and draws on the children's experiences as they undertake the activities and the ensuing discussion.

Let us imagine that the children in the class have experience of cross country type events in the school grounds. The teacher now sets them a task to be conducted in pairs. The children, A and B, individually plan a 4 control cross country event with an agreed start and finish point. They write control descriptions for each other. The control sites and descriptions are checked by the teacher and the controls are set out.

A now tackles B's course and vice versa. Afterwards they discuss the courses they set, the problems involved and the accuracy of the control sites. Time was not taken in this instance. The

emphasis was on course setting, the location of the controls, accurate descriptions and finding the controls. The compass was used throughout to maintain orientation.

Let us apply the INFORM framework again. The first act is to identify the SoA. This time there are several, spanning across four subject areas.

AT1	Geog 3b	Use a large-scale map to locate their own position and features outside the classroom
AT4	Math 3c	Use the 8 points of the compass to show direction
AT4	Math 4b	Specify location
AT1	Math 4a	Identify and obtain information necessary to solve problems

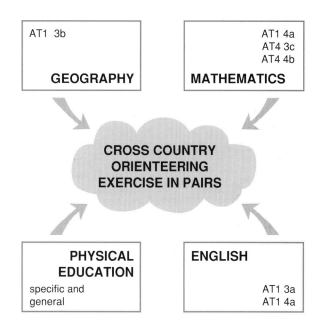

Statements of Attainment related to a cross country orienteering exercise

Key Stage 2 PE (general)	Respond safely, alone (and with others) to challenging tasks Evaluate how well they and others perform and behave against criteria suggested by the teacher and suggest ways of improving performance
Key Stage 2 PE (specific)	Experience competitions, including those they make up themselves

ORIENTEERING: CHILD'S NAME . . . . DATE OF BIRTH . . . .

GEOGRAPHY

STATEMENT OF ATTAINMENT LEVELS: KEY STAGES 1 AND 2

ATTAINMENT TARGETS	1	2	3	4	5	6
AT1 GEOGRAPHICAL SKILLS	1a Follow directions	2a Use geographical language	3b Use a large scale map	4b Measure distance	5b Interpret relief maps	6f Use map and compass to follow a route
	1b Observe and talk about a familiar place	2b Make a representation of a place	3c Make a map of a short route	4f Draw a sketch map		
		2c Follow a route using a plan	3d Identify features on air photographs			
AT2 KNOWLEDGE & UNDERSTANDING OF PLACES	1a Name familiar features of the local landscape		3c Use correct geographical language			
AT5 ENVIRONMENTAL GEOGRAPHY		2b Describe how the environment has changed	3a Describe the effect of extracting different resources	4b Discuss whether special protection is needed		
		2c Suggest how the environment could be improved		4c Describe how damaged land can be restored		

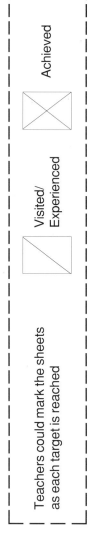

Visited/Experienced

Achieved

Teachers could mark the sheets as each target is reached

MATHEMATICS

	1	2	3	4	5	6
AT1 USING AND APPLYING MATHEMATICS	1b Talk about their work and ask questions	2a Select materials and mathematics for a practical task	3a Find ways of overcoming difficulties in problem solving	4a Identify and obtain information to solve problems	5a Carry through a task by breaking it down	
	1c Make predictions based on experience	2b Talk about work using appropriate mathematical language	3b Use appropriate mathematical terms	4b Interpret situations mathematically using symbols and diagrams	5c Make a generalisation and test it	
		2c Respond to "What would happen if...?"		4d Make generalisations		
AT2 NUMBER	1a Use numbers in context	2c Identify halves and quarters	3d Make estimates based on familiar units of measure	4a Solve problems without calculator	5b Find fractions and percentages of quantities	
	1b Add and subtract	2d Recognise the need for standard measures		4e Make sensible estimates of a range of measures	5d Use units in context	
AT4 SHAPE AND SPACE	1a Talk about models they have made	2a Use mathematical terms to describe shape and objects	3a Sort shapes using criteria	4a Construct 2D and 3D shapes and know associated language	5c Use networks to solve problems	6c Understand and use bearings to show direction
	1b Follow or give instructions related to movement and position	2b Recognise different forms of movement	3b Recognise reflective symmetry	4b Specify location		
	1c Compare and order objects without measuring		3c Use eight points of the compass to show direction			
AT5 HANDLING DATA	1a Sort a set of objects describing criteria chosen	2a Interpret relevant data	3a Access information in a simple database	4c Use the mean on a range of data		6a Design and use a questionnaire to survey opinion

PHYSICAL EDUCATION

		GENERAL	ATHLETIC ACTIVITY	OUTDOOR AND ADVENTUROUS ACTIVITY
PE KEY STAGE 1		Practise and improve performance	Experience and take part in running	Explore the potential for physical activity within the immediate environment
	1d	Recognise the effect of physical activity on their bodies		Undertake simple orientation activities
		Describe what they and others are doing		Develop an awareness of basic safety practices
PE KEY STAGE 2	2b	Perform effectively in activities requiring quick decision making	Practise and develop basic actions in running	Learn the principles of safety in the outdoors and develop the ability to assess and respond to challenges in a variety of contexts and conditions
	2c	Respond safely, alone and with others, to challenging tasks taking account of levels of skill and understanding	Experience competitions including those they make up themselves	Experience outdoor and adventurous activities in different environments that involve planning, navigation, working in small groups recording and evaluating
	2e	Evaluate how well they and others perform and behave against criteria suggested by the teacher and suggest ways of improving performance		Be taught the skills necessary for the activity undertaken with due regard for safety including the correct use of equipment
	2f	Be able to sustain activity over appropriate periods of time and understand the immediate and short term effects on the body		

ENGLISH

STATEMENT OF ATTAINMENT LEVELS: KEY STAGES 1 AND 2

	1	2	3	4	5	6
AT1 SPEAKING & LISTENING	1c Respond appropriately to simple instructions given by the teacher	2d Describe an event, real or imagined 2d Talk with the teacher, listen and ask questions	3d Give, receive and follow accurately precise instructions when pursuing a task individually or as a member of a group	4a Give a detailed account, or explain why a particular course of action was taken	5d Contribute to the planning of, and participation in a group presentation	
AT3 WRITING			3d Produce a range of types of non chronological writing	4c Organise non chronological writing for different purposes in orderly ways	5d Assemble ideas on paper or on a VDU, individually or in discussion with others Show evidence of an ability to produce a draft from them, to revise and redraft as necessary	

6   A community project

Let us now assume that the pupils are confident in the basic skills and knowledgeable and experienced in a particular location, say the school grounds. How can this work be extended and present benefits for others? Is it possible to generate a project which allows the benefits of orienteering to be given to the local community while presenting children at Key Stage Two with a real challenge which would embrace other curricular areas?

THE SETTING UP OF AN ORIENTEERING COURSE IN A LOCAL PARK

Taking part in an orienteering event requires one level of skill, but making maps, setting problems for others, and monitoring and evaluating the activity raises the level of skill to a much higher standard.

There are many things that pupils could do. They could set line, cross country or score events for other pupils within their own class or within the school. If that was successful, they could put on a small-scale event for another school in the locality. However, the scheme we now consider takes orienteering into the community. It is ambitious but not beyond the scope of primary children. It involves the setting up of a number of controls - say 20 to 30 - in a local area, and the production of a map which will be made available to the public. The aim would be to explore the area, locate the controls and receive feedback and reward for the completion of the activity, the whole being organised and/or administered by the school.

The controls could form either a cross-country course or score course, as described earlier. However, we can suggest a further variation - a TRIM event. This event originated in Sweden. The TRIM event challenges individuals, groups and families to use the map to find all the controls marked on it. There is no time limit. It could be completed in a day or over a number of visits to the area.

On completion of the course the control card, which was obtained with the map from the school, is returned and checked. Certificates can be awarded according to success. The actual control sites could be signs or even nesting boxes high on trees but visible from pathways. Code letters and numbers could be painted on the sides. If markers were used, these could be relocated after a period of time to present new challenges.

The figure opposite shows how the core and foundation subjects are linked by the cross-curricular skills, themes and dimensions to present an integrated topic web. Each aspect of the web is shown in the chart on page 56 in greater detail.

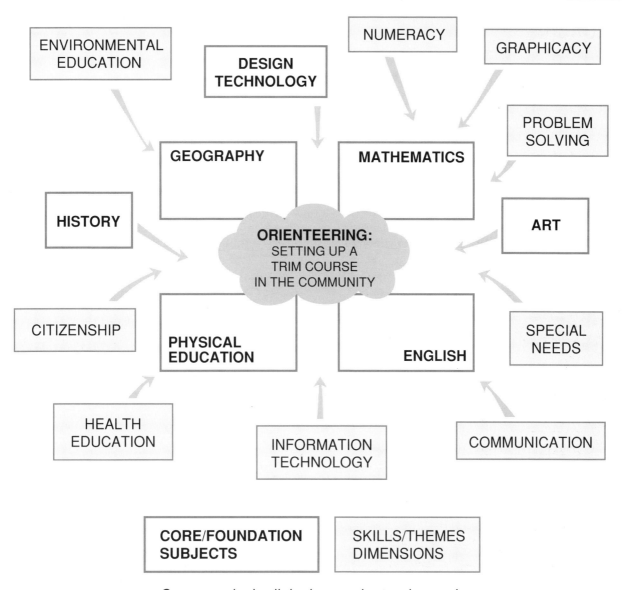

ENVIRONMENTAL EDUCATION

DESIGN TECHNOLOGY

NUMERACY

GRAPHICACY

PROBLEM SOLVING

GEOGRAPHY

MATHEMATICS

HISTORY

ORIENTEERING: SETTING UP A TRIM COURSE IN THE COMMUNITY

ART

CITIZENSHIP

PHYSICAL EDUCATION

ENGLISH

SPECIAL NEEDS

HEALTH EDUCATION

INFORMATION TECHNOLOGY

COMMUNICATION

CORE/FOUNDATION SUBJECTS

SKILLS/THEMES DIMENSIONS

Cross curricular links in an orienteering project

SUMMARY

This topic is challenging but realistic. You may be able to adapt the idea for your own school grounds. Orienteering equips you with skills to tackle problems and challenges within unknown terrain. The community project would present opportunities and difficulties to be solved, but if accomplished would provide considerable benefit to local people and great satisfaction to the instigators. It would be a big step, but you are not alone, for you now have a map (of the curriculum) to guide you.

Some of the contributions of orienteering to aspects of learning and cross curricular competencies are shown overleaf.

GEOGRAPHY

- Survey the area, check features on the ground
- Extract information from existing maps
- Draw maps
- Decide location of controls

MATHEMATICS

- Use compass and scale to check the position of features
- Consider scale for the maps, having concern for users
- Collect, interpret and present data on use of the course over a trial period

COMMUNICATION

- Develop the basic idea through discussion
- Persuade and negotiate for permission
- Write instructions for the event
- Produce press handout, publicity material
- Report the progress of the venture
- Role play to explore how people will react
- Interview participants who test the event
- Produce questionnaire on reaction to the event
- Tape-record immediate reaction
- Word process the report

HISTORY

- Explore existing maps
- Discuss what changes have taken place
- Was it always like this?
- What detail from conventional maps should be excluded ?

DESIGN TECHNOLOGY/EXPRESSIVE AND AESTHETIC CONSIDERATIONS

- Design and produce a map using up to 5 colours
- Consider siting of title, key, control card, scale and information
- Design and produce control markers
- Design and produce instruction sheet
- Set up a system for the distribution and collection of control cards and instructions
- Agree roles within the organisation
- Produce publicity material, signs, posters and displays advertising the activity
- Design and produce certificates of completion

PROBLEM SOLVING

- Identify potential problems related to people using the facility
- Identify any potential environmental problems

SPECIAL EDUCATIONAL NEEDS

- Consider the problems faced by people with special needs
- Can the map be held by people who have to walk with aids, the wheelchair bound, the young or the elderly?

INFORMATION TECHNOLOGY

- Set up a database of users

CITIZENSHIP

- Encourage a sense of fair play, a sense of responsibility to others for the management of the event and participation within it

ENVIRONMENTAL

- Discuss the need for maintenance of the course and equipment
- Encourage adherence to the Country Code and good behaviour in the countryside

HEALTH AND FITNESS

- Consider the safety implications of the activity for different abilities and age ranges
- Consider the health and fitness benefits from regular exercise

7 Games

1 MATCHING PAIRS

• Measure out 10 boxes on each sheet of card, each one about 6cm x 8cm.

• Draw in neatly 10 symbols and 10 written descriptions.

• Cut out.

This game can be used by individuals or pairs sitting down and matching the symbols cards with the description cards or as a running game with the cards at different ends of a hall or playground, start from the middle of the hall.

> EQUIPMENT
> Two sheets of different coloured card
> Black, orange, blue, green crayons or felt pens
> Scissors

2 CONTROL FEATURE IDENTIFICATION

• Select 10 different features - line features plus buildings and colours.

• Draw control circles round each feature.

• Number 1 - 10 on a piece of paper

The children have to write the correct feature in each circle. This can be done sitting or running.

> EQUIPMENT
> A variety of orienteering maps
> Circle template, red pen, paper

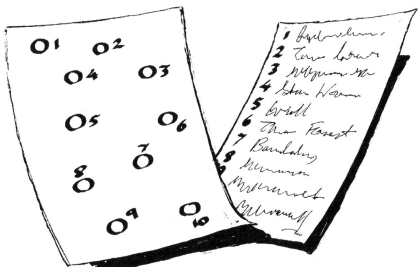

More games can be found in Start Orienteering Book 6. Ready made sets of game cards and dominoes for symbol recognition are available from Harveys (see Appendix B, page 64).

8 Orienteering beyond the school

Orienteering offers a variety of experiences outside school both as a competitive sport and as recreational relaxation. This chapter contains details of opportunities. This is not exhaustive but hopefully will give a flavour of orienteering as an absorbing pastime which can extend classroom interest into enthusiasm for the Great Outdoors.

The resource section in Appendix B contains further sources of information, equipment suppliers, and details of books and manuals, including "Teaching Orienteering", which offers a comprehensive guide for teachers.

PERMANENT COURSES

Permanent courses are the orienteering equivalent of running tracks or sports halls. They offer a valuable resource for school, club and community coaching and training.

Essentially, a permanent course is a scatter of marker posts set in a park, wood or forest section and shown by the usual numbered circles on an orienteering map. Some urban maps may be simple in the extreme and the courses may require the participants to weave between fences or buildings. Forestry Commission Courses sometimes still use the term "Wayfaring" and show runnable forest as green on the map instead of white. The posts are usually moved at regular intervals to avoid the creation of a new path network between controls.

Used imaginatively, permanent courses can offer much more than a score type introduction to orienteering, but like all sports halls they require experienced and qualified coaches and leaders to bring out their full potential as an orienteering resource. Many of the exercises in this Teacher Guide can be used on permanent courses and we also list the following which are particularly effective, in that they save 'teacher' energy and time in setting out and retrieving markers as well as giving control of the activity.

1. Controls can be permutated for introductory handrail courses.

2. Star exercises for team competitions or compass exercises

3. Team or individual score events

4. Compass and distance judgement exercises

5. Relocation exercises

Most of these exercises can give technical and physical training even where the area is well known to the participants. A school programme, involving all the ideas mentioned above, could realistically be planned and carried out on one permanent course. A comprehensive list of permanent courses in the UK is available from the British Orienteering National Office. This includes contact addresses and map outlets.

COLOUR CODED EVENTS

Colour Coded Events are cross-country orienteering competitions intended to cater for all levels of orienteering ability. Courses are designated by colour, where each colour represents a course with a certain level of physical and technical difficulty (generally the darker the colour the longer or harder the course). This ensures a consistency of course standards between events so that someone entering an Orange course one weekend will be able to enter an Orange Course the following weekend in a different area confident that the physical and technical standards will be similar.

A youngster is expected to start on either the White or Yellow course, whilst an adult novice begins with either the Yellow or Orange course, depending on his or her confidence. Progression can then be made either towards longer courses with the navigation remaining relatively simple, or onto technically difficult courses up to the appropriate length for the individual level of fitness.

The shorter courses with a low level of technical difficulty (White and Yellow) will be mainly along paths so the terrain and technical difficulty will have only a small effect on competitors' times. More difficult courses will demand compass, route choice and contour skills and could involve steep climbs and rough terrain. The level of difficulty will influence guidelines on time.

Colour awards

A White Award can be made to anyone who completes three White courses.

The Colour Coded Standard for courses other than White is either the time that is achieved by at least 50% of those who started the course (including the retirals and disqualifications), or 150% of the winner's time - whichever gives the largest number of qualifiers. The Controller has discretion to extend the qualifying time, but not to reduce it.

A competitor qualifies for a colour award (other than White) by attaining the Colour Coded Standard for that course on three separate occasions.

Pairs can qualify for colour awards on the White, Yellow and Orange courses.

Colour Coded Course Guidelines

Time (mins) for most competitors	15-35	24-45	35-60	45-75	55-90	65-105	75-120
Length (km)	1.0-1.5	1.5-2.5	2.5-3.5	3.5-5.0	5.0-7.5	7.5+	10.0+
Technical difficulty / Physical difficulty — Control sites	1	2	3	3	4	5	5
1 — Major line features and junctions	White						
2 — Line features and very easy adjacent features		Yellow					
3 — Line features + easy point features close to lines			Orange	Red		Purple	
4 — Minor line and easy point features			Light Green				
5 — Small point + contour features				Green	Blue	Brown	Black

Learn orienteering step by step

Level 1   Understanding the map, getting used to being in the woods
            Orientating the map using the terrain
            Map colours and the most commonly used symbols
            Orienteering along a single path

Level 2   Orienteering from path to path
            Reading objects by paths
            Navigating by line features

Level 3   Shortcuts
            Taking controls just off paths
            Orienteering on short legs against catching features
            Distance judgement
            Making simple route choices

Level 4   Rough orienteering on longer legs against catching features
            Fine orienteering using short legs
            Understanding contours
            Orienteering using large knolls and significant re-entrants

Level 5   Reading contours in detail and at competition speed
            Using the correct techniques with changes in difficulty
            Longer legs and longer distances to catching features
            Pacing
            Difficult control points

CHECKLIST FOR ORGANISING AN ORIENTEERING EVENT

1. Choose an appropriate area and get written permission for access. Draw up budget if appropriate.

2. The map - check scale - detail - accuracy

3. Plan armchair course(s) and check on the ground. Arrange for a second opinion to control the event. Tape control points.

4. Choose an organisation team of adequate experience - start: finish: results computation and display

5. Equipment - Markers - Punch - Control Cards - Start/Finish Signs - Taped Finish - Tent - Tables - Results Display

6. Safety procedures
Establish and communicate to organisation team and competitors

7. Prepare master maps/overprint course on maps - map corrections, control description sheets. Any other instructions.

8. Set out course well in advance and have it checked by controller. Arrange for dismantling and clearing up afterwards

9. Debrief and send out results

10. Prepare for next event

Orienteering organisation eats up time
- plan every stage well in advance -

SAFETY CODE FOR ORGANISERS OF ORIENTEERING EVENTS

Orienteering is not especially hazardous (DES Safety in Outdoor Education booklet)

1. Build safety into course planning
A suitable area - Collecting Features - Handrails - Checkpoints - Clearly Marked Out of Bounds Areas

2. Participants and organisers
Must have the right degree of experience and knowledge of maps and basic navigation techniques - beginners take part in pairs

3. Retirement procedure
Everyone must know - put it on control description sheet - with time limit.

4. Start and finish manned throughout
Match finishing competitors' control cards with stubs from the start to ensure everyone is back.

5. Emergency system
Whistle - Watch - Time Limit - Systematic Pre-planned Search System - Safety Bearings (if appropriate) First Aid - EVERYONE MUST KNOW.

6. Ensure adequate equipment for conditions
Protection against cold, wind and rain - stout footwear with grip, gloves if cold, drinks if hot, map cases etc.

ABOVE ALL . . . .

7. The difficulty of the course must be appropriate to the age, skills, fitness and experience of the participants.

9 Developing personal performance

BOF Coaching Award Scheme

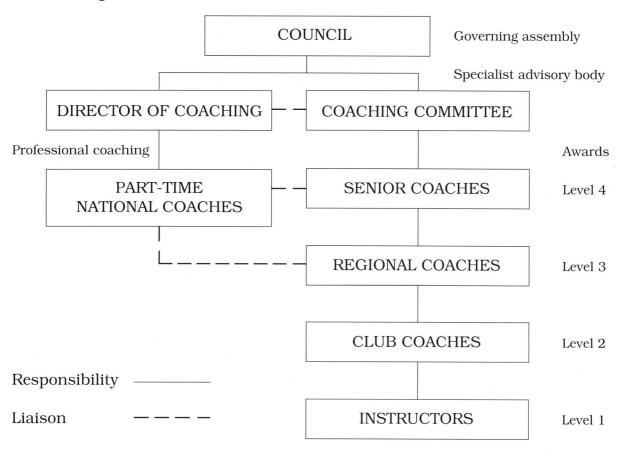

The British Orienteering Federation's Coaching Award Scheme is designed to help orienteers of all ages and levels of ability to realise their full potential through a uniform system of instruction and thereby enhance their enjoyment of the sport. The scheme is divided into four levels.

Level 1: Instructor
The award is aimed at teachers, youth leaders, outdoor activity instructors and any others involved in introducing orienteering, mainly to young people.

Level 2: Club coach
This coach works with beginners and less experienced orienteers of all ages at club level.

Level 3: Regional coach
The coach is involved with personal performance at regional and national level, trains and assesses candidates for level 1 and 2 awards.

Level 4: Senior coach
The holder of this award is an expert in orienteering who may have responsibility for a specific area of coaching at national level. He/she contributes to the running of courses, National Squad coaching, the development of coaching techniques and the generation and dissemination of coaching ideas.

Full qualification and assessment conditions for each level of award can be obtained from the BOF National Office. Detailed information on coaching, physical training and orienteering techniques is contained in the Federation's Training and Coaching manuals. The Federation's coaching activities are co-ordinated by a full-time Director of Coaching, who has responsibility for part-time National Coaches who fill specific posts within the scheme.

The personal performance ladder

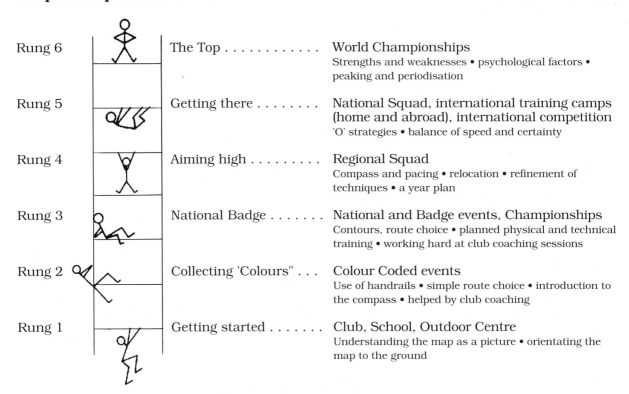

Rung 6	The Top	**World Championships** Strengths and weaknesses • psychological factors • peaking and periodisation
Rung 5	Getting there	**National Squad, international training camps** **(home and abroad), international competition** 'O' strategies • balance of speed and certainty
Rung 4	Aiming high	**Regional Squad** Compass and pacing • relocation • refinement of techniques • a year plan
Rung 3	National Badge	**National and Badge events, Championships** Contours, route choice • planned physical and technical training • working hard at club coaching sessions
Rung 2	Collecting 'Colours" . . .	**Colour Coded events** Use of handrails • simple route choice • introduction to the compass • helped by club coaching
Rung 1	Getting started	**Club, School, Outdoor Centre** Understanding the map as a picture • orientating the map to the ground

Incentive schemes are an important part of the sport and exist at different levels. The colour coded system has succeeded in combining competition of graded technical and physical difficulty with cheap on-the-day entry for all levels of competition at local events.

The national 'Badge' scheme awards iron, bronze, silver, gold and championship badges after three events have been completed within a time based on the average of the first three in each class, e.g. gold = average of first three +25%, silver = average of first three + 50%, etc.

The Scottish Orienteering Association has long run a scheme where '5', '10' and '20' badges can be gained after completing the appropriate number of timed events. This has proved an excellent scheme for beginners.

Orienteering is one of 15 sports within the CCPR Pentathlete Scheme for children aged from 5 to 16 years and a new National Navigation Award uses orienteering skills as the basis of a progressive navigation badge scheme.

A full fixture list and details of incentive schemes are available from the BOF National Office. The fixture list is included in CompassSport and in a quarterly BOF News which is sent to all Federation members.

Competitions and incentive schemes are designed to provide the motivation for individuals to improve their orienteering techniques and overall personal competence. The figure above shows a personal performance ladder and indicates the route to the top for the ambitious orienteer.

Supporting the growth and development of personal competence is a National and Junior Squad structure and a comprehensive coaching scheme.

The Senior Squad aims directly at preparation for World Championships and, with the help of Sports Council funds, provides a programme of home and overseas courses and competitions tailored to the short and long term plans of individual members, each of whom has a personal coach.

The Junior Squad seeks to identify outstanding young orienteers in Britain and to develop their technical ability so as to provide a foundation of good orienteers upon which Britain's international programme can be built.

Home competition programmes and overseas links and training camps have produced a dramatic improvement in the performance of both junior and senior teams.

Twelve regional squads cater for juniors with potential who wish to develop their skills and physical fitness. These squads, catering for the 13-17 age groups, organise weekend courses and in some cases overseas training.

APPENDIX A

School maps

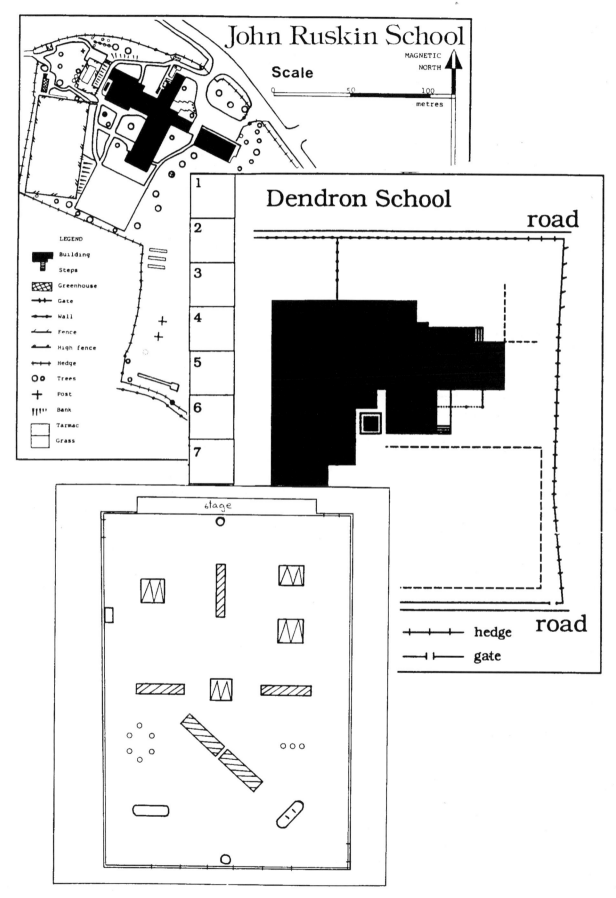

ORIENTEERING IN THE NATIONAL CURRICULUM

APPENDIX B

Resources and information for teachers, instructors and coaches

BOOKS & PAMPHLETS

Start Orienteering
by Carol McNeill and Tom Renfrew (Harveys).
A series of books of lesson plans for teachers.
Book 1 (6-8 year olds) ISBN 1 85137 0404
Book 2 (8-9 year olds) ISBN 1 85137 0501
Book 3 (9-10 year olds) ISBN 1 85137 0331
Book 4 (10-12 year olds) ISBN 1 85137 0609
Book 6 Games & exercises ISBN 1 85137 0803

Teaching Orienteering
by Carol McNeill, Jean Ramsden and Tom Renfrew (Harveys).   Comprehensive manual containing over 100 lesson plans.
ISBN 1 85137 020X

The Coaching Collection
by Peter Palmer and Jim Martland (BOF).

Fun With Orienteering
by Jo and Tony Thornley (Kaye & Ward).

Guidelines for Course Planning
(International Orienteering Federation).

Orienteering Training and Coaching
(British Orienteering Federation)
ISBN 0 95022 8133

Skills of the Game - Orienteering
by Carol McNeill (Crowood Press).
ISBN 1 85223 5586

Back to Basics
by Peter Palmer (Harveys).
To be published January 1993.

The DNS/Silva Protractor Compass
by Jim Martland and Sue Walsh.
Forthcoming 1993.

Orienteering Rules and Guidelines
British Orienteering Federation 1992

Mapmaking for Orienteers
by Robin Harvey (Harveys).
ISBN 1 85137 0013

Compass Sport: 37 Sandycoombe Road, Twickenham, Middlesex, TW1 2LR.
Magazine for orienteers, 8 issues per annum. Subscriptions: 25 The Hermitage, Eliot Hill, London, SE13 7EH: Tel. 081 852 1457

Most of the books opposite are obtainable from Harveys (address below):

Harveys: 12-16 Main Street, Doune, Perthshire, FK16 6BJ. Tel: 0786 841202. Fax: 0786 841098
• Largest supplier of teaching resources, materials, books, videos and other audio-visual aids; introductory packs and technique training worksheets; equipment for organising orienteering (see back cover).
• Mapmaking service, including map printing.
• Free catalogue available.

Ultrasport: The Square, Newport, Salop, TF10 7AG. Tel: 0952 813918
Orienteering clothing, equipment and shoes. Ultrasport offers discounts for club and school group orders.

Silva UK Ltd: Unit 10 Sky Business Park, Eversley Way, Egham, Surrey, TW20 8RF Tel: 0784 471721
Silva offer a range of orienteering equipment and kit, as well as the world renowned Silva compasses. Discounts are available for club and school group orders.

Orienteering Services (Martin Bagness): 2 Gale Crescent, Lower Gale, Ambleside, Cumbria, LA22 0BD. Tel: 09394 34184
Map drawing; instruction/coaching for orienteering courses at all levels.

British Orienteering Federation, Riversdale, Dale Road North, Darley Dale, Matlock, Derbyshire DE4 2JB. Tel: 0629 734042 (24 hour answering service). Fax: 0629 733769
BOF has introductory packs for individuals, clubs and schools, information on member-ship, permanent courses, coaching awards, schools schemes and fixtures. A limited number of videos are available on loan. A quarterly BOF News is sent to all members and affiliated organisations. A Coaching Newsletter is issued at regular intervals to all coaches who qualify through the BOF Coaching Award Scheme.

International Orienteering Federation, PO Box 76, S-191 21 Sollentuna, Sweden
IOF Scientific Group produces a twice yearly research journal.